THE GENIUS
OF THE
JEWISH JOKE

THE GENIUS OF THE JEWISH JOKE

ARTHUR ASA BERGER

illustrated by the Author

JASON ARONSON INC.
Northvale, New Jersey
London

The author gratefully acknowledges permission to reprint from the following sources:

An Anatomy of Humor by Arthur Asa Berger. Copyright © 1993 Transaction Publishers. Reprinted by permission of Transaction Publishers.

Humor 4-2 (1991), article by Avner Ziv. Copyright © 1991 MOUTON DE GRUYTER, a Division of Walter de Gruyter & Co.

This book was set in 12 pt. Garamond Book by Alpha Graphics of Pittsfield, New Hampshire.

Copyright © 1997 Arthur Asa Berger

10 9 8 7 6 5 4

All rights reserved. Printed in the United States of America. No part of this book may be used or reproduced in any manner whatsoever without written permission from Jason Aronson Inc. except in the case of brief quotations in reviews for inclusion in a magazine, newspaper, or broadcast.

Library of Congress Cataloging-in-Publication Data
Berger, Arthur Asa, 1933–
    The genius of the Jewish joke / Arthur Asa Berger.
       p. cm.
    Includes bibliographical references and index.
    ISBN 1-56821-977-6 (alk. paper)
    1. Jewish wit and humor—History and criticism. I. Title.
PN6231.J5B367   1997
809.7'35203924—dc20   96-27144
                                                          CIP

Manufactured in the United States of America. Jason Aronson Inc. offers books and cassettes. For information and catalog write to Jason Aronson Inc., 230 Livingston Street, Northvale, New Jersey 07647.

This book is dedicated to my wife,
Phyllis Wolfson Berger

Contents

Preface	xi
1 How Is This Book about Jewish Humor Different from All Other Books about Jewish Humor?	1
The Passover Seder	1
How Is This Book Different?	2
Why Do We Laugh? How Do You Explain Humor?	3
What Makes Us Laugh? A Different Approach	4
An Aside on Three Aspects of Humor	5
What, or Is It Who, Are the Jews?	8
Distinguishing Characteristics of Jewish Humor	10
Avner Ziv on the Main Characteristics of Jewish Humor	13
On the Significance of the Yeshiva for Humor	15

Jewish Humor and Jewish Identity	20
Conclusions	23
2 How Odd of God to Choose the Jews	**25**
On the Nature of Jokes	25
On the Form of Jokes	28
The Ten Commandments Joke	31
A Radical Hypothesis: A Biblical Explanation of Why the Jews Are Such a Humorous People	32
More Speculations on Jewish Humor	35
A Psychoanalytic Explanation: Why the Jews Are Such a Comic People	37
Political Cultures and Jewish Jokes	42
3 On the Techniques of Jewish Jokes	**47**
Functions of Jewish Humor	47
Anti-Negro Jokes and Triumphant Victims	51
Using the Forty-Five Techniques to Analyze a Joke	56
Theorists of Humor and the Tan Joke	60
Who's Right about the Tan Joke?	63
On Humorous Techniques and Power	63
Conclusions	80
4 Schlemiels, Schlimazels, and Other Jewish Fools and Comic Types (Old World and New World)	**83**
On Jewish Types in Jokes and Folklore	83
On the Humor of Types	85

Jewish Dialect in Jewish Jokes	87
The Schlemiel	92
The Schlimazel	97
The Shadken	101
The Schnorrer	104
An Aside on American Jewish Humor and Kinds of Congregations	108

5 Jokes about Jews and Ethnic and Racial Minorities — 111

Jokes about Jews by Non-Jews	112
Italian Jokes that Italian-Americans Tell about Themselves	121
Elephant Jokes as Disguised Anti-Negro Jokes	123
Polish Stereotypes	125
Light Bulb Jokes	127
Why the Riddle?	131
On Jewish Jokes and Jokes about Jews	133

6 On the Question of Masochism and Other Aspects of Jewish Humor — 137

The Question of Masochism	138
Reik on Jews as Schlemiels	144
On ErosGOPanalia and Idi Amin: Two Personal Examples	148
Humor and the Jews	150
Some Distinctive Aspects of Jewish Humor	154
Conclusions	158

Glossary of Yiddish Terms	161
Bibliography	165
Index of Names	171
Index of Topics	173
Index of Jokes	181

Preface

Humor is an enigma that has engaged, fascinated, and perplexed the most brilliant minds humanity has produced, from Aristotle to Freud, from Kant to Bergson. Our greatest philosophers and psychologists have tried to figure out why we laugh and have offered numerous ingenious explanations of humor. Not only has humor interested our philosophers and psychologists (and other kinds of "deep thinkers"), this mysterious thing called humor has attracted and been used by many writers and other creative artists. It permeates the work of our most brilliant playwrights and filmmakers. We find wonderful dramatic comedies written by Aristophanes, Plautus, Shakespeare, Ben Jonson, Oscar Wilde, Eugene Ionesco, Tom Stoppard, Neil Simon, Woody Allen, and countless others. Many of the world's greatest novels are comedies, as well.

Humor also is part of our everyday lives: we read comics and cartoons in newspapers and magazines, we watch situation comedies, we go to films that are comedies, we make witty remarks from time to time, and, most important of all for my purposes, we tell jokes.

If humor is an enigma, Jewish humor is particularly enigmatic. How do you explain the existence of Jewish humor, given the experiences of the Jews over the centuries? How is it that Jews have laughed and seen the world from a comic perspective in the face of persecutions, pogroms, the Holocaust, endemic anti-Semitism, and so on? This book explains what I describe as the *genius* of the Jewish joke—what is distinctive about it, its unique character and spirit, its association with Jewish character and culture, and its relationship to Jewish survival. Some Jewish jokes are very old, but many are very *au courant* and deal with contemporary matters, as we see in the two jokes that follow:

Pleasure from My Son
Two little old Jewish ladies are walking down the street. "Oy, my son," says one. "He's a source of displeasure, but he's also a source of pleasure."

Preface

"How is he a source of displeasure?" asks the other woman. "He's a homosexual." "And how is he a source of pleasure?" asks the other woman. "He's going with a doctor!"

The Captain

A Jewish man makes a lot of money and buys a big boat. He invites his mother and father aboard to take a cruise. When they come aboard they see he's wearing a hat with "Captain" on it. When she sees the cap, the mother says, "By me you're a captain and by your father you're a captain. And by you you're a captain. But by a captain are you a captain?"

Jewish jokes, as we will see, have many different functions, reveal many interesting things, and are often viewed in different ways by different people. Jokes are often double-edged: a joke can serve as a source of pleasure for some people (who tell a joke about Jews or Blacks or women or whomever) as well as a source of displeasure for other people (the people about whom the joke is being told). But the "victims" of jokes often take pleasure in them as well as the "victimizers."

This first joke doesn't mean anything unless you recognize the significance doctors play in American Jewish society and culture. There are numerous Jewish jokes about Jewish mothers trying all kinds of things to marry their daughters off to doctors. The old woman's son may not be a doctor, but he's going with a doctor, which is the next best thing. The second joke alludes to the question of assimilation, which will be dealt with in more detail in a later chapter.

The Genius of the Jewish Joke is about Jewish jokes and, by implication, Jewish humor and Jewish culture. Many of the books on Jewish humor are really books *of* Jewish humor that offer examples of Jewish humor—selections from folklore, jokes, short stories, and novels—with a little bit of history and explanation here and there. There are, in addition, a number of scholarly and analytical books about Jewish humor and Jewish jokes. In this book, I concentrate on Jewish jokes, riddles, and related forms, which means, technically speaking, the book is about Jewish oral humor or popular Jewish humor or what might be described as Jewish folk humor.

That is more than enough for a book. If I wished to cover Jewish humor in short stories, novellas, novels, plays, movies, radio, television, cartoons, and comic strips, in America and elsewhere, in the present era and in earlier times, it would take a series of books or a truly gigantic one.

Let me offer, here, a classic Jewish joke about one of the great heroes of modern Jewish history and culture—physicist Albert Einstein.

The Question of Relativity
An old Jewish man reads about Einstein's theory of relativity in the newspaper and asks his son to explain it to him. "It's really complicated, but let me explain it to you this way," says the son. "You know how the time flies if you're with someone you really like, but if you touch your finger to a hot stove, a second seems to last forever?" "I understand," says the old man, nodding his head. "But tell me, this Einstein ... from this he's making a living?"

Preface

In this book I reprint a number of jokes, often modifying them a bit from printed versions (which often vary considerably in different books) to make them stronger and easier to understand. Many of the Yiddish terms, I should point out, are spelled in different ways by different authors, so you'll see a number of different spellings for terms such as schlemiel and schlimatzl. I offer a glossary at the end of the book in which I define the Yiddish terms used in the jokes, for those who are not Jewish or don't know Yiddish or both.

I believe I can get to the essence of Jewish humor by focusing my attention on Jewish jokes. Others have felt the same way, for there are a half dozen or so books devoted to Jewish jokes and a large number of books devoted to Jewish humor.

I've written a good deal on humor myself over the last thirty years and must confess there are those who would say that much of what I write is humorous—or, as they might put it, what I write "should not be taken seriously." For example, a number of years ago I saw a poster at San Francisco State University announcing that a women's group was having a meeting dealing with becoming e-mancipated. It led me to write an article for *The San Francisco Sunday Examiner*, "The Significant HE," in which I asked whether the terms *he* or *men* or *man*, which are part of many words women use for themselves, were not, in fact, brainwashing them and causing them to remain subservient to men.

I pointed out that words such as *menstruate*, *menopause*, *female*, and *she* all have what we might call linguistic masculinities hidden inside them. Then I asked (showing that I am a feminist), Why are there Manischevitz matzos and not Womanischevitz matzos? Why Hebrew and not Shebrew? Why hedonist and not shedonist? Why heinous and not sheinous? Why history and not herstory? (Some feminist writers do use the term *herstory* now.) I ended my article by reminding my readers that there is a discipline that explains how language shapes our beliefs—se*man*tics.

There is one other thing I should mention here. Jokes are often terribly insulting to members of ethnic, racial, sexual, religious, and other groups. Let me apologize, in advance, for using the jokes I do, some of which are truly repellent (but all of which, I believe, are funny and significant). That is part of the genius of humor and of jokes: they are often ugly, tasteless, and politically incorrect, but they represent a kind of fearlessness and audacity that makes humor the liberating force that it is, or can be. If I confined myself to "tasteful jokes" (that may be an oxymoron), I'd be severely limited.

I have provided a glossary at the end of the book in which I list and define Yiddish terms that are found in many Jewish jokes, but I can only offer a limited amount of information. You have to know something about the Jews and Jewish culture and society to appreciate certain Jewish jokes and Jewish humor. If, for example, you did not know that Manischevitz is a prominent maker of matzos and other Jewish foods, my wordplay above about Womanishevitz would be meaningless.

We are now ready to begin our investigation of Jewish jokes and Jewish humor and, by implication, Jewish culture. And lingering in the background, of course, the inescapable (for Jews) matter of the Jewish question!

1

How Is This Book about Jewish Humor Different from All Other Books about Jewish Humor?

If you aren't Jewish, the title of this chapter won't mean very much to you, except that it might seem rather long and convoluted, with claims to uniqueness of dubious validity. If you are Jewish, or if you know anything about Jewish holidays, you'll recognize this as a parody of the famous "question" that children are asked to answer during the Passover Seder.

THE PASSOVER SEDER

In this combination religious observance and feast, the youngest child is asked a question and, in turn, asks four questions:

How is this night different from all other nights?

1. On all other nights we eat either leavened bread or unleavened bread (matzos); on this night why only unleavened bread?
2. On all other nights we eat herbs of any kinds; on this night, why only bitter herbs?
3. On all other nights we do not dip our herbs even once; on this night, why do we dip them twice?
4. On all other nights we eat our meals in any manner; on this night why do we sit around the table together in a reclining position?

The Seder, which means order, tells the story of the escape of the ancient Jews from the Pharaoh in Egypt and offers contemporary Jews an opportunity to relive the experience existentially. Jews all over the world read the Passover Haggadah—a guidebook that tells them how to conduct the Seder service. The Passover Seder is, in essence, the answer to these questions. During the Seder, a goodly amount of wine is consumed and, at the end, funny songs are sung, so we have the combination of sadness and happiness, a bittersweet quality that some have found in much Jewish humor.

Let me point out, also, that this is one of the earliest examples of another trait which is supposedly common to Jews—answering a question with a question. In this case, four questions.

HOW IS THIS BOOK DIFFERENT?

This book is, like the Passover Seder, an answer to the question I posed in the title of the chapter. My focus, you will see, is not only on the subjects dealt with in Jewish humor but also with the techniques found most commonly in Jewish humor and, in particular, in certain Jewish jokes that I happen to like very much and which I think are representative and significant.

But before I start analyzing Jewish humor, I would like to say something about humor in general.

WHY DO WE LAUGH? HOW DO YOU EXPLAIN HUMOR?

These questions have, as I pointed out in my preface, perplexed philosophers and deep thinkers for centuries. Why anyone laughs is a mystery. Aristotle is supposed to have written a book on humor that has been, most regrettably, lost. Many of the greatest philosophers, such as Hobbes, Kant, and Bergson, tried to explain why we laugh, and the same holds true for psychologists, psychiatrists, linguists, political scientists, sociologists, and so on.

There are probably hundreds of theories of humor, and one book I own, Ralph Piddington's *The Psychology of Laughter: A Study in Social Adaptation*, lists dozens of theories elaborated by thinkers such as Locke, Rousseau, Descartes, Hegel, Schopenhauer, Spencer, Darwin, and Freud. (Freud's book, *Jokes and Their Relation to the Unconscious*, has a number of excellent Jewish jokes in it.)

Generally speaking, there are four dominant theories of humor, and all the other theories fall under them. The first theory argues that humor is based on some kind of incongruity—that is, what we get is not what we expect; the second theory argues that humor is based on a sense of superiority (in the person laughing); the third theory,

Freud's psychoanalytic theory, suggests that humor involves masked aggression (and is also connected to various economies in psychic expenditure). The fourth theory, which I would describe as a cognitive theory, ties humor to the way the mind processes information and the creation of play frames that indicate that what is being recounted is not to be taken seriously.

WHAT MAKES US LAUGH? A DIFFERENT APPROACH

I have elaborated, in a number of articles and books, a different approach to humor—one that doesn't ask why we laugh (we probably will never find out) but asks what makes us laugh. I made a content analysis of all the humor I had in my house a number of years ago—of comic books, books of jokes, books of Jewish folklore, plays by every-

LANGUAGE	LOGIC	IDENTITY	ACTION
Allusion	Absurdity	Before/After	Chase
Bombast	Accident	Burlesque	Slapstick
Definition	Analogy	Caricature	Speed
Exaggeration	Catalog	Eccentricity	
Facetiousness	Coincidence	Embarrassment	
Infantilism	Comparison	Exposure	
Insults	Disappointment	Grotesque	
Irony	Ignorance	Imitation	
Misunderstanding	Mistakes	Impersonation	
Over literalness	Repetition	Mimicry	
Puns/Wordplay	Reversal	Parody	
Repartee	Rigidity	Scale	
Ridicule	Theme and	Stereotype	
Sarcasm	Variation	Unmasking	
Satire			

Figure 1.1. Categories and Techniques of Humor

one from Shakespeare to Ionesco, books of humorous verse, short stories, novellas, and novels, and so on—and came up with what I suggest are the forty-five techniques of humor that all humorists use, in various permutations and combinations.

I will be using these techniques to analyze a number of Jewish jokes, to see what they reveal about how these jokes generate humor and what they reflect about Jews and Jewish culture. I should point out that some scholars do not like this typology (one scholar called my typology "inelegant") and argue that I confuse categories in it. My answer is that it is reasonable to consider styles such as parody and satire as techniques; one parodizes and one writes satirically. It may be that some of my categories, such as burlesque, are too broad, but for all practical purposes what I have elaborated in my list of techniques enables us to understand how humorists generate laughter better than any other method I am familiar with.

We know, I would say, what makes people, in general, laugh. And we can find out how humorists, in all media, working in all genres, create humor (even if they can't explain things themselves). But is there anything unusual about what makes Jews laugh? Why should Jews, a "despised people," as some have put it, have such a remarkable sense of humor?

AN ASIDE ON THREE ASPECTS OF HUMOR

One of the basic techniques of humor, as the figure above shows, is disappointment and defeated expectations. A subcategory of that is going off on tangents in shaggy-dog jokes and interrupting what seems to be the logical order of things. As a humorist, as well as a scholar of humor, I claim the right to go off on tangents from time to time.

There are, let me suggest, three ways to look at humor and its rewards. These are found in the chart below:

Haha	Laughter and Pleasure
Ahah	Discovery and Pleasure
Ah	Triumph and Pleasure

"Haha" represents an involuntary (though desired) response we make to jokes and other forms of humor that generate sudden laughter. "Ahah," on the other hand, suggests a kind of discovery through humor of some important insight. "Ahah" is an inversion of "Haha," and the focus is not on a sudden burst of laughter (which may be connected to insult and aggression, for example) but on an epiphany, a sudden discovery of some relationship between things we had not seen before. "Ah" represents a sense of relaxation, of well-being, of success, perhaps even a sense of triumph in some respect.

All three may be found in the same joke or "text" (to use the jargon of contemporary literary theory). When you find all three in a joke, you have, I would suggest, a very fine joke. Not only a fine joke, but a profound joke. Not only a profound joke, but probably a very profound joke.

Consider the following joke, which is repeated in most books of Jewish humor:

You're Right!
A man comes to a rabbi's house and asks the rebbetzin, "Can I see the rebbe? It's most urgent." The

rebbetzin shows the man in to see the rabbi. The man then recites a litany of complaints about his wife. As the man speaks, the rabbi nods his head in agreement. "Yes, yes . . . you're absolutely right." This gives the man great comfort, and he leaves. A short while later, the man's wife comes in and demands to see the rabbi. She is in a state of great excitement. So the rebbetzin shows the woman in. "I'm here about my husband," she tells the rabbi. Then she lists a number of complaints about her husband. As she talks, the rabbi nods his head and says "Yes, yes . . . you're right." The woman calms down, thanks the rabbi, and leaves. Then the rebbetzin comes in and says to her husband, "I don't understand you. When the man came, you agreed with everything he said. Then his wife came and contradicted everything the man said, and you agreed with her. You're on both sides of the same argument." The rabbi nodded his head and said "Yes, yes . . . you're right."

In this joke, it is true that the rabbi agreed with two people who had diametrically opposite views, and his wife saw this and called him on it. What she didn't recognize, it is suggested, is that the rabbi's main concern was in calming each of the excited partners down and giving them some comfort. This joke has all three of the general kinds of humor in it: laughter, discovery, and success (triumph over adversity). It also shows that human qualities are more important, in many cases, than logic or legalism.

WHAT, OR IS IT WHO, ARE THE JEWS?

The Jewish answer to this question is, "Why do you want to know?" But logic tells us that we should come to some conclusions about who and what Jews are, in order to understand Jewish jokes and humor. Deciding who is and who isn't Jewish, or who isn't *really* Jewish, is not an easy matter, by any means.

Two Bees
Two bees, Mike and Melvin, are flying through the air. One of them, Melvin, is wearing a Yarmulkah. "Why are you wearing a Yarmulkah?" asks Mike. "I don't want to be mistaken for a WASP," replies Melvin.

First of all, we have to recognize that Jews are people who practice, with varying degrees of following the rules, Judaism, the Jewish religion. Technically speaking, according to the Jewish religion, any person born to a Jewish mother is Jewish. (People who are not born to a Jewish mother but convert are also Jewish, though Orthodox Jews don't consider conversions by Reform Rabbis and maybe even Conservative Rabbis to be valid.)

I would suggest that if people don't identify themselves as Jewish and don't practice Judaism, whether they are the children of a Jewish mother or not, they are not Jewish. It helps if, in addition to identifying oneself as Jewish, one practices Judaism (even if only to a minor extent) and one is raised in what might be described as Jewish culture. This involves such things as religious practices, dietary observances, instruction in Jewish beliefs, and so on.

Let me offer an example that involves religious practices. To make sense of this joke, it is important to know that Orthodox Jews have a rule that says men and women are not allowed to dance together. At weddings, the men dance with other men and the women dance with women. Let me add that Conservative Jews and Reform Jews do not have this rule.

No Dancing Allowed
A young Orthodox Jew is getting married and he asks his rabbi, "Could you possibly allow me to dance with my wife after we're married?" "No," says the rabbi. "That's forbidden." So the young man asks the rabbi a question about having sex. "Would it be okay for us to have sex on the rug?" "Perfectly fine," says the rabbi. "What about having sex on a sofa?" "That too is fine," says the rabbi. "And while sitting on a chair?" "Yes, if you like to do it that way," says the rabbi. "What about having sex while standing?" "No, no!" says the rabbi. "Then you'd end up dancing together."

This joke is obviously a Jewish joke—it involves Jews, rabbis, and Orthodox Jewish religious practices. Not all Jewish jokes have to be so obviously Jewish, but there has to be something Jewish about the events in the joke and the people involved in the joke for a joke to be a Jewish joke.

Second, I would say that Jews are often described as a "people," a group of people who have something in common. Jews descend from the ancient Hebrews and thus have a unique ancestry. Jews are not a racial group—there are Jews in many different races. But Jews all have a religion in common and, despite considerable differences, some common cultural attributes generally tied to their religion and various customs, practices, and dietary prescriptions that are connected to it. Jews are sometimes called "people of the book," the book being the Torah, the first five books of the Old Testament.

Third, Jews are commonly understood to be an ethnic group—a rather loose term used to describe people who belong to some religious, racial, cultural, or national group. The term *ethnic* is derived from the Greek term *ethnikos*, nation. Thus we talk about Jewish-Americans in the same manner we talk about Italian-Americans, Polish-Americans, Irish-Americans, and in recent years, African-Americans (though not all black people in America are from Africa).

Finally, with the emergence of Israel as a nation-state, Jews living in that country now can be said to have a nation, and many Jews who don't live in Israel (Jews are scattered all over the world) nevertheless have very strong emotional ties to the State of Israel and support it politically and financially.

If Jews are found in many different countries and are raised speaking different languages (and often speaking in different accents in a given language), how can one talk about Jewish humor? I have Jewish friends from Great Britain who were educated at Oxford and Cambridge and most certainly do not speak with what is generally held to be a "Jewish" accent. (Jewish accents in England are often quite different from Jewish accents in America.) My friends speak with the "received pronunciation," though their identification with Judaism is very strong.

DISTINGUISHING CHARACTERISTICS OF JEWISH HUMOR

In order to deal with Jewish humor, we have to have a working definition of what it is. I will rely on that given by Avner Ziv, an Israeli scholar who has done a considerable amount of work on Jewish humor over the years. In the Introduction to a special edition of *Humor: International Journal of Humor Research*, which Ziv edited, he writes (1991, 145):

> Jewish humor is the humor created by Jews, reflecting aspects of Jewish life. This broad definition includes popular verbal humor, such as jokes, or anecdotes (collected by folklorists), as well as humor created by professionals. Therefore, popular Jewish jokes collected by folklorists, Shalom Aleichem's writings, and parts of Neil Simon's plays and Woody Allen's movies are all examples of Jewish humor. Since humor reflects a people's life, it changes and varies accordingly. Thus one can talk about Eastern European, Sephardic, American, or Israeli Jewish humor. In spite of the great differences in the life conditions of these different communities, Jewish humor has certain characteristics which make it unique. What is generally identified in the professional literature as Jewish humor originated in the nineteenth century, mainly, but not exclusively, in Eastern Europe. Today, in the USA, Jewish humor is considered one of the mainstreams of American humor, and a couple of decades ago 80 percent of the most successful humorists were Jewish (Janus 1975).

Ziv makes a number of important points in this passage that are worth considering.

First, he suggests that Jewish humor is humor created by Jewish people. That seems to be rather obvious, but there is humor about Jews that is not created by Jews—a subject I will deal with in a later chapter. Second, Ziv includes both popular humor and humor made by professionals in his definition of Jewish humor. Thus we must include jokes, anecdotes, plays, films, and all other forms of humor, popular as well as elite.

Ziv also argues that Jewish humor is distinctive and unique, despite the fact that Jews come from many different countries and have different life experiences. Jewish humor also reflects the way Jewish people live, and as the way they live changes, so does the humor. Finally, he quotes an amazing statistic: in the 1970s in America, 80 percent of the successful humorists were Jewish. Since Jews represent about 3 percent of the population in the United States, they were overrepresented as humorists by a factor of more than twenty-five.

Jews, I should add, are overrepresented in many different areas. I once saw a program with a half dozen leaders of different religions on it, and most of them were Jewish—at least originally. That is what gives the following joke such resonance.

The Abbott

A little old lady from Brooklyn takes a plane to India, on her way to a meeting with the head abbot of a monastery high in the mountains. She lands in Calcutta and takes another plane to the base of the mountain and then hires Sherpas to help her make the steep ascent to the monastery where the esteemed abbot is in residence. She finally reaches the monastery and is met by a junior abbot. "His holiness will receive you," the junior abbot says, "but you can only say three words to him." The woman is ushered into a large room, at the end of which, on a platform high above everyone, sits the head abbot in the lotus position. On the floor of the room numerous devotees of the abbot sit, deep in prayer. She walks down a long passageway, led by the junior abbot, and up many stairs until she is standing on a platform below the head abbot. "Remember," says the junior abbot, "only three words." The woman gazes at the abbot, her eyes full of love. She opens her mouth and says, "Seymour, come home!"

This joke deals, in a humorous way, with the problem of assimilation that troubles many Jews. Why is it, they ask, that so many Jews become Zen Buddhists, Hare Krishnas, or whatever, when they can find the same kind of spirituality in Judaism, which has a very strong mystical component? The name of the hero of this tale, "Seymour," also identifies the story as a Jewish one, since that is a name that was commonly used by Jewish people in earlier years.

AVNER ZIV ON THE MAIN CHARACTERISTICS OF JEWISH HUMOR

Ziv also deals with what he considers to be the main psychological characteristics of Jewish humor, which are, he suggests (*Humor*, 1991, 146):

1. An intellectual dimension: a desire to distort the reality, to alter it and make it laughable (and thus less frightening and threatening). Reducing the awful reality into absurdity is a cognitive process by which one tries to make life more tolerable.
2. A social dimension: trying to maintain internal cohesiveness and identity. By comparing "us" with "them" it is pos-

sible to show that even if in reality "they" are stronger, "we" can still win, mainly by using our wits.
3. An emotional aspect: helping one to see oneself as one is, namely far from perfect. Making fun of some unsavory aspect of one's behavior and personality might help in accepting them. It can even show that they are not so terrible: the proof—I can even laugh at them. Another emotional aspect related to self-disparagement is the sympathy one earns from others, and being accepted is, and was for two thousand years, a serious problem for a wandering people.

Ziv alludes to a number of aspects of Jewish humor that are worth considering in more detail. His first point, about making reality more manageable, is not unique to Jewish humor, for all humor has this effect. But Jewish humor, more than many other kinds of humor, does so because of the social and political "reality" that the Jews faced—being a despised minority in a generally hostile society. This marginality of the Jews is, I would suggest, one of the major factors behind the development of the Jewish comic sensibility, a matter Ziv alludes to when he talks about Jews being a "wandering people."

On the general level, humor offers individuals a means of resisting suffering and guilt and the need to repress their impulses, sexual desires, and drives—a repression that Freud described as the "discontents" of civilization. Because Jews tend to be highly moralistic, one can argue that their sense of guilt is rather acute, which would explain why Jews, generally speaking, have such an elaborated comedic sensibility.

There is a famous joke that alludes to the Jewish penchant for joking.

Nationalities and Jokes

If you tell a joke to an Englishman, he will laugh three times: first, when you tell the joke; next when you explain it; and third, when he understands it. If you tell it to a Frenchman, he will laugh twice: first, when you tell the joke; and second, when you explain it. He will never understand it. If you tell the joke to a Russian, he will laugh once: when you tell it, for he won't let you explain it and he'll never understand it. It you tell a joke to another Jew, however, he will not laugh at all. Before you are halfway through, he'll interrupt you, shouting, "That's an old one. Besides, I can tell it better."

The Jew didn't laugh because he had heard the joke before, not because he didn't have a sense of humor. Once we have heard a joke, it no longer has the ability to make us laugh—unless we forget it and the punch line.

ON THE SIGNIFICANCE OF THE YESHIVA FOR HUMOR

As "people of the book," Jewish humor, especially absurd Jewish humor, also provides Jews with an escape from what might be described as "the prison-house of logic," an escape from the limitations of rational thought and intellectual rigor. Interestingly enough, it is the tradition of rational thought that is connected to much Jewish humor. In the yeshivas (schools) of Eastern Europe, young

Jewish children engaged in *pilpul*, a very high level, sophisticated analysis of the Torah.

In *Life Is with People: The Culture of the Shtetl*, Mark Zborowski and Elizabeth Herzog describe education in the yeshivas (1952, 97–98):

> The general principle of the yeshiva is independence and self-reliance. The program of study allows for infinite variation. The basic study is exhaustive analysis of the Talmud and its commentators. In addition, each student is privileged to spend a large share of his time on the part of Jewish wisdom that appeals to him. If he is attracted by mystical problems, he will study the *kabala*; if philosophy is his field, he will delve into the works of the philosophers . . . Talmudic study is often called *pilpul*, meaning pepper, and it is as sharp, as spicy, as stimulating as its name implies. It involves comparison of different interpretations, analysis of all possible and impossible aspects of the given problem, and—through an ingenious intellectual combination—the final solution of an apparently insoluble problem.
>
> Penetration, scholarship, imagination, memory, logic, wit, subtlety—all are called into play for solving a talmudic question. The ideal solution is the *khiddush*, an original synthesis that has never before been offered. This mental activity is a delight both to the performer and to his audience. Both enjoy the vigor of the exercise and the adroitness of the accomplishment.

Let me suggest that this kind of training can generate not only rabbis and religious scholars but also comedy writers and comedians (as well as linguists, literature professors, and lawyers). A comedian's stand-up routine can be seen, without pushing things too far, I would suggest, as a secularized version of the *khiddush*. Many Jewish jokes deal with the remarkable logical ability of Jews, as the following joke shows.

Jewish Logic

After months of negotiation, a Jewish scholar from Odessa was granted permission to visit Moscow. He boarded a train and found an empty seat. At the next stop, a young man got on and sat next to him. The scholar looked at the young man and thought: This fellow doesn't look like a peasant, and if he isn't a peasant, he probably comes from this district. If he comes from this district, he must be Jewish because, after all, this is a Jewish district. On the other hand, if he is a Jew, where could he be going? I'm the only one from the district who has permission to travel to Moscow. Wait—just outside Moscow there is a village called Samvet. He's probably going to visit someone there, but how many Jewish families are there in Samvet? Only two—the Bernsteins and the Steinbergs. The Bernsteins are a terrible family, so he must be going to visit the Steinbergs. But why is he going? The Steinbergs have only girls, so maybe he's their son-in-law. But if he is, which daughter did he marry? Sarah married that nice lawyer from Budapest, and Esther married a businessman from Zhadomir, so it must be Sarah's husband. Which means that his name is Alexander

Cohen, if I'm not mistaken. But if he comes from Budapest, with all the anti-Semitism they have there, he must have changed his name. What's the Hungarian equivalent of Cohen? Kovaks. But if he changes his name, he must have some special status. What could it be? A doctorate from the university. At this point he turned to the young man and said, "How do you do, Dr. Kovacs?" "Very well, thank you," answered the startled passenger. "But how did you know my name?" "Oh," replied the scholar, "it was obvious." (Novaks and Waldoks, 1981, 2)

The same mentality that would have led a person to become a rabbi or scholar in the shtetl (where education and intelligence were the most highly valued attributes a person could have) leads secularized Jews to become writers, humorists, comedians, and comediennes. But despite the "freedoms" of American culture and society, Jews still remain very marginal, numerically, and Jewish humorists often reflect this marginality.

Our earliest Jewish humor in America was an immigrant humor, as immigrants from Eastern Europe came to America to escape persecution (the pogroms of Poland and Russia, for example) and to create a future for themselves and their children. Since they were outsiders and experienced anti-Semitism here (how ironic), their choice of occupations was severely limited. Thus, relatively speaking, a considerable number of Jews became entertainers—a profession that was looked down upon by most people at the time. (There were even a significant number of Jewish boxers at one time.)

This Eastern Europe heritage is the source of the various Jewish dialect jokes that were so popular. This dialect was spoken by the first generation of Jewish immigrants; we do not find it in contemporary Jewish humorists such as Jack Benny, Sid Caesar, Woody Allen, or Andrew Dice Clay. And many contemporary Jewish jokes do not rely on accents to identify themselves as "Jewish."

This accent is the source of ambivalence in many Jews, who are ambivalent about their ethnic identity or religio-ethnic identity. One generation behind the sophisticated surgeon, professor, or lawyer are parents from Russia or Poland who speak with an accent. The Jewish accent suggests an incomplete assimilation into American culture and society . . . and perhaps, at an unconscious level, a refusal to completely assimilate, to lose one's "old world" identity and become Americanized. In contemporary American society, maintaining one's ethnic identity is now considered desirable and politically correct; but in earlier times, the ideal was to become Americanized, which meant, in essence, becoming WASPs—white Anglo-Saxon Protestants.

A "Jewish" accent is not a sure indicator that we have a Jewish joke, for many anti-Semitic jokes use this accent as a means of ridiculing and heaping scorn on Jews and suggesting that Jews are not really Americans the way the joke tellers (who may be Irish-Americans, Italian-Americans, Polish-Americans, German-Americans, and so on) are. We are a nation of immigrants, though many of us would like to forget this fact. In fact, even though maintaining one's ethnic identity is considered good, many universities offer courses in getting rid of an accent. So accents plague new generations of immigrants the way they did older generations, except that now we tend to be less tolerant of accents as signifiers of "difference" and being "not completely American."

Humor becomes a tool for criticizing society and "getting away with it." As a minority, Jews have a vested interest in making sure that the government protects them (and other minorities as well) and use humor as one means of helping maintain democratic institutions and calling attention to injustices of all kinds. Jewish humor has a survival dimension to it, and Jews survive by using their wits in more ways than one.

JEWISH HUMOR AND JEWISH IDENTITY

There is also an element of identity reinforcement in Jewish humor: many Jewish jokes allude to Jewish customs, dietary proscriptions, history, cultural practices, and identity. In doing so, they serve the purpose of helping "define" Judaism and reinforce Jewish identity—even though they may use Jewish comic types and customs as the sources of their humor.

As American Jews become more and more assimilated and lose hold of Jewish customs, culture, and their Jewish identities, one can only wonder whether Jewish humor will change and more or less disappear—along with the Jews. In America, the intermarriage rate between Jews and non-Jews is now around 50 percent, and many of the children of these marriages are not raised as Jews. At that rate, the Jews will become a much smaller minority in America than they are now; there will be a small group of Orthodox Jews and remnants of Conservative and Reform Jews.

The subject of intermarriage and assimilation is also the matter of a famous Jewish joke.

The Rabbi's Son and the Shiksa
A rabbi's son come homes one day and announces that he is going to marry a shiksa (a gentile girl) and that, in addition, he is going to convert to Christianity and become an Episcopalian. The rabbi goes into his study and prays to God. "Dear God," he prays. "My son is going to abandon Judaism, become a Christian, and marry a gentile girl. Where did I go wrong?" God hears the rabbi's prayer and answers him. "You think you're having trouble with your son. Look at my *son!"*

This theme of a minority group losing its identity is not unique to the Jews. Relatively large percentages of Japanese-American women marry "out"—that is, they marry Caucasians, perhaps, among other things, as a means (unconscious, I would imagine) of escaping from their sense of marginality.

There is another Jewish joke that deals with assimilation.

Mr. Cohen, I Presume?
On a flight to New York from San Francisco, four men happened to end up in the first-class lounge of a Boeing 747. They began to chat. After ten or fifteen minutes, one of the men said, "allow me to introduce myself. My name is Jack Collins."

> The second man said, "My name is Albert Cole." The third man said, "My name is Martin Cowan." Then the fourth man said, "Isn't that a remarkable coincidence? My name used to be Cohen also."

Here we find the matter of Jewish identity, in particular, Jewish names, being the subject of the joke. It alludes to the way many American Jews "Americanize" their names and, in so doing, hide or disguise their identities as Jews. The joke also reflects the stereotype that Jews tend to be affluent, since they are all in the first-class lounge of the airplane.

Let me offer one more joke, which gives us an ironic commentary on the matter of intermarriage.

> **The Convert's Dilemma**
> A young Jewish girl, Heather Katz, falls in love with a guy named Bill Smith, a shaygits (non-Jewish male). But Heather won't marry Bill unless he converts to Judaism. So he decides to do so. He goes to a rabbi, receives instruction in the Jewish faith, and becomes a Jew. After a while, Heather decides she doesn't love Bill anymore, and calls the marriage off. "What should I do?" Bill asks Heather's father. "Heather isn't going to marry me!" "Why not do what many Jewish boys do nowadays—marry a shiksa!"

This joke is a study in comic irony: Bill, a Christian, becomes a Jew to marry the woman he loves, who then dumps him. When he asks her father for advice, he suggests, in a bittersweet reversal, that Bill marry a shiksa, a gentile woman, which means he's really back where he started.

Finally, let me quote a riddle that also deals, in a zany way, with the topic of Jewish identity and interracial intermarriage.

The Fruits of Intermarriage
Question: What do you get if you cross a Jew with an African-American?
Answer: A janitor. But he owns the building.

This riddle uses negative stereotypes of Jews and African-Americans to create humor, suggesting that such marriages are ultimately destructive. The term "cross" suggests one is dealing with animals and conducting some kind of breeding experiment. The black part of the child that is born becomes a janitor, but the white part of him involves being well-to-do and thus owning the building he's janitor in.

CONCLUSIONS

There are several factors that I suggest are found in Jewish jokes and Jewish humor of all kinds, factors which are perfectly logical and not surprising. First, Jewish humor often has a religious content to it; that is, it deals with rabbis, God, Judaism, and its various practices and beliefs. There is a preoccupation with Jewish identity and the dangers of assimilation. Secondly, Jewish humor deals with Jewish people and their relations with other Jews or with Jews and their relations with Jews and non-Jews. Jewish humor and Jewish jokes without Jews in them seem hard to imagine, though I imagine anything is possible. There are all kinds of comic Jewish types who are found in Jewish humor and Jewish jokes. Third, Jewish humor reflects what might be described as a Jewish mentality or sensibility tied to the Jewish religion and caused by Jewish marginality and the fact that Jews have been forced to wander all over the globe. This sensibility tends to be very moral, concerned with social justice and democracy—though it also is often quite absurd.

Some have suggested that Jewish humor is masochistic and excessively self-critical, a subject I will deal with in more detail elsewhere in this book. I would argue that this is not the case at all. If Jewish humorists use "victim" humor, it is because they come from a people that has been greatly victimized over the centuries and they are members of a highly marginal group, so they do not operate from a position of power.

There are, I would suggest—and I'm oversimplifying things somewhat—two kinds of Jewish humor: Old World Jewish humor from the shtetl and from the earliest immigrants to America, and New World humor, created by second- and third-generation American Jews. We will see this split in much of the humor that will be analyzed in later chapters.

2

How Odd of God to Choose the Jews

The title of this chapter refers to the fact that the Jews are known as the "chosen" people. What does it mean that Jews are the chosen people? People who do not like Jews or do not know the Bible use this term to suggest that Jews feel superior to other people and other religions—those who were not "chosen." In reality, the term refers to the fact, as Jewish theologians explain things, that the Jews were chosen by God to receive the Torah (and with the Torah, the Ten Commandments). The Jews receiving the Ten Commandments has become the subject of a very famous joke that I will offer after a digression on the nature and formal properties of jokes.

ON THE NATURE OF JOKES

Before I tell this joke, I should say something about what a joke is. A joke is conventionally defined as *a relatively brief narrative or story, meant to evoke mirth and laughter, with a punch line.* This punch line, always a surprise, always unsuspected in good jokes, is what generates the laughter. The existence of punch lines suggests freedom from logic and rationality and has implications for people as far as their lives and mental health are concerned. We are, jokes tell us, free, and life is full of surprises. Change is always possible. We also use the term *joke* to cover other forms of humor that are not, strictly speaking, jokes: "Polish jokes," which are actually riddles, and also amusing anecdotes and stories. I will accept this latitudinarian understanding of jokes, even though most of the time the jokes I recount will be real jokes.

The distinguished British social anthropologist Mary Douglas explains this matter in her article "Jokes" (*Implicit Meanings*, 1975, 96):

> A joke is a play upon form. It brings into relation disparate elements in such a way that one accepted pattern is challenged by the appearance of another which in some way was hidden in the first. I confess that I find Freud's definition of the joke highly satisfactory. The joke is an image of the relaxation of conscious control in favour of the subconscious.... The joke merely affords opportunity for realizing that an accepted pattern has no necessity. Its excitement lies in the suggestion that any particular ordering of experience may be arbitrary and subjective. It is frivolous in that it produces no real alternative, only an exhilarating sense of freedom from form in general.

If we add to Douglas' notion the idea that jokes show that any particular ordering of society is arbitrary, we can see how jokes have a subversive significance, even if they do not offer alternatives to the societies, events, or elements in these societies they are ridiculing.

Douglas acknowledges this when she writes (1975, 95) that "what is important" in jokes is that "one accepted pattern is confronted by something else" and that all jokes have a "subversive effect on the dominant structure of ideas."

She makes another interesting point relative to the relationship that exists between jokes and society. As she explains (1975, 98):

> My hypothesis is that a joke is seen and allowed when it offers a symbolic pattern of a social pattern occurring at the same time. As I see it, all jokes are expressive of the social situations in which they occur. The one social condition necessary for a joke to be enjoyed is that the social group in which it is received should develop the formal characteristics of a "told" joke; that is, a dominant pattern of relations is challenged by another. If there is no joke in the social structure, no other joking can appear.

What this means is that jokes are intimately connected to the societies (or elements of societies) in which they are found, which explains why jokes do such a good job of revealing beliefs and attitudes.

In a sense, a joke that people tell reflects or depicts, indirectly, the "joke" (the absurd relationships, the silly things people do, human foibles, and so on) that exists in the society where the joke is told. Jokes work, Douglas adds, only when they mirror social forms. We can see, then, why jokes are so valuable. Jokes seem, at first sight, to be trivial— but they have the power to reveal important things about the societies in which they are found and what might be described as "the human condition," as well.

ON THE FORM OF JOKES

A joke has the following form (each letter represents what might be called a "jokeme," a part or segment of the joke):

$$A \to B \to C \to D \to E \to F \text{ (punch line)}$$
$$\downarrow$$
$$G \text{ (laughter)}$$

F in this joke is the punch line, and G represents laughter, mirth, whatever you will. For example, consider the following joke.

A Lesson in Arithmetic
A man from Chelm marries a woman and three months after their marriage she bears a child. Perplexed, the man goes to the rabbi. "I married this woman and three months after we were married she had a baby." "Ah," said the rabbi. "You don't understand such things. First, how long has it been since you married your wife?" "Three months," said the man. "And how long has it been since your wife married you?" "Three months," said the man. "And how many months has it been since you have been married?" asked the rabbi. "Three months," said the man. "That makes nine months!" said the rabbi.

A in my chart would represent the first part of the joke, "A man marries a woman and three months after they were married she has a baby." B would represent the next part, "Perplexed, the man goes to his rabbi." Each letter would represent another part of the joke, and the length of the joke would determine the number of letters in the diagram. Finally, F would represent the punch line, where the rabbi says "That makes nine months."

This joke contains a wonderful perversion of logic, as the rabbi strives to comfort the man and convince him that everything is all right. We must remember that Chelm is, in Jewish folklore, a town of fools, so that establishes the play frame that makes the joke possible. The man is revealed as a typical Chelmian simpleton who didn't recognize that his wife was six months pregnant when he married her. It also reveals that the citizens of the shtetls, fools and nonfools, were sexual beings who often strayed from the straight and narrow path.

A riddle, such as the one I told earlier that asks "what happens when you cross a Jew with an African-American?" is not, technically speaking, a joke. The very language of this riddle, "what happens when you cross . . . " comes from animal husbandry and is used for breeding dogs or horses or cows. Comic riddles, as I understand them, are questions that tend to be zany and lead to humorous answers. It is possible to see riddles, I would suggest, as shortened forms of jokes and to use the "answer" part of riddles as punch lines. Thus the riddle about crossing African-Americans with Jews could be retold as a joke:

The Janitor
"Did you hear what happened when Bessie Cohen married a shvartze?" "No." "They had a son—he ended up as a janitor. But unlike most janitors, he also owns the building."

This joke is stronger as a riddle, but I think you can see how it is possible to turn riddles into jokes.

It is important to recognize that jokes are only one form of humor and that many of our greatest humorists don't tell jokes but create humorous stories that use the various techniques listed in my chart of the forty-five techniques of humor: exaggeration, parody, insult, facetiousness, and so on. Jokes are useful, however, because they are short enough to reproduce (so readers can see for themselves what one is writing about) and because they often reflect important concerns.

When we tell jokes, we are really performing someone else's material. Some people do a great job at this, and others don't. But a person who amuses us by telling jokes created by others isn't, I would argue, a funny person but, instead, is an excellent performer. The same thing applies to actors and actresses in plays. They may have roles that are hilarious, but that doesn't mean that they are, as individuals, funny. Usually, of course, people who tell jokes well have a good sense of humor and may use their theatrical gifts to enhance the quality of the jokes they tell.

This leads to an important insight. One can tell a joke a number of different ways, as long as the substance of the joke is kept and the punch line works. That is, names can be changed, and the words in the joke can be modified, but the sense of the joke must be maintained. That is why you often see a joke told in slightly different ways. Jokes are orally transmitted texts, though later they are often written and published in books.

With all of this in mind, let us turn to the famous Ten Commandments joke.

THE TEN COMMANDMENTS JOKE

This is generally considered a classic Jewish joke. It deals with a part of the Jewish religion and also uses the stereotype that Jews are "cheap" and always looking for bargains. It merges these two strands together to "explain" how the Jews got the Ten Commandments and thus became the "chosen" people.

The Ten Commandments
God comes down to Egypt one day and says to the Egyptians, "I have a commandment, and I'd like to give it to you." "What's the commandment?" ask the Egyptians. "Thou shalt not commit adultery!" "No thanks," say the Egyptians. Then God goes to the Assyrians and says, "I have a commandment, and I'd like to give it to you." "What's the commandment?" ask the Assyrians. "Thou shalt not commit adultery!" replies God. "No thanks," say the Assyrians. Then God goes to Moses and says, "I have a commandment, and I'd like to give it to you." "How much does it cost?" asks Moses. "Nothing," says God. "Then I'll take ten," says Moses.

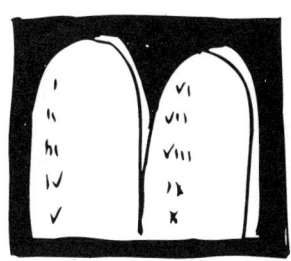

Notice in this joke that Moses doesn't ask what the commandment is but how much it costs. When he finds out it doesn't cost anything, he asks for ten of them. This joke can be seen as a kind of parody of biblical stories. Notice also that this joke shows God taking three tries to get someone to accept his commandment(s). We often find the number three in jokes. It is, as Alan Dundes has pointed out, a dominant number in European and American culture, but not in all cultures.

A RADICAL HYPOTHESIS: A BIBLICAL EXPLANATION OF WHY THE JEWS ARE SUCH A HUMOROUS PEOPLE

I've already suggested that the training that Jews had in the yeshivas and the practice of *pilpul* sharpened their wits and made it relatively easy for them to transfer their intelligence and sophisticated understanding of language from religious pursuits to creating humor.

Let me now suggest that the Torah offers an interesting insight into the relationship of Jews and humor. In the Torah, we find an important story that has significance for Jewish humor. In Genesis 17:27, we find God telling Abraham that he will become a father.

> And God said to Abraham, "As for your wife Sarai, you shall not call her Sarai, but her name shall be Sarah. I will bless her; indeed, I will give you a son by her. I will bless her so that she shall give rise to nations; rulers of people shall issue from her." Abraham threw himself on his face and laughed, as he said to himself "Can a child be born to a man a hundred years old, or can Sarah bear a child at ninety?" And Abraham said to God, "Oh that Ishmael might live by Your favor!" God said, "Nevertheless, Sarah your wife shall bear you a son, and you shall name him Isaac; and I will maintain my covenant with him as an everlasting covenant for his offspring to come."

In the next portion we find that Abraham was ninety-nine years old when he was circumcised and Ishmael was thirteen years old when he was circumcised, and both were circumcised on the same day. In the next chapter, Genesis 18:32, Abraham is sitting under his tent and sees three men coming toward him. He tells Sarah to make cakes and set some food before the three men.

Let me quote again, because it is pertinent to my hypothesis.

> They said to him, "Where is your wife Sarah?" And he replied, "There, in the tent." Then one said, "I will return to you when life is due, and your wife Sarah shall have a son!" Sarah was listening at the entrance of the tent, which was behind him. Now Abraham and Sarah were old, advanced in years; Sarah had stopped having the periods of women. And Sarah laughed to herself, saying "Now that I am old and withered, am I to have enjoyment—with my husband so old?" Then the LORD said to Abraham, "Why did Sarah laugh, saying 'Shall I in truth bear a child, old as I am?' Is anything too wondrous for the LORD? I will return to you at the time that life is due, and Sarah shall have a son." Sarah lied, saying "I did not laugh," for she was frightened. But He replied, "You did laugh."

Sarah laughs, just as Abraham did, for neither of them believed it was possible for them, at such advanced ages, to have a child. The interplay between Sarah and God about whether she laughed or not is somewhat remarkable, mirroring the kind of bickering we find in many humorous relationships.

I will skip the story of Sodom and Gomorrah and move to Genesis 21, in which Sarah conceives.

> Sarah conceived and bore a son to Abraham in his old age, at the set time of which God had spoken. Abraham gave his new-born son, whom Sarah had borne him, the name of Isaac. And when his son Isaac was eight days old, Abraham circumcised him as God had commanded him. Now Abraham was a hundred years old when his son Isaac was born to him. Sarah said "God has brought me laughter; everyone who hears will laugh with me."

It is important for us to know that *Isaac* means "laughter." Thus we have, at one of the most important points in Jewish history, from the union of Abraham and Sarah, the first Jews, a strong association between laughter and the Jewish people.

In Genesis 22, we find God decides to put Abraham to the test in the famous sacrifice story.

> Some time afterward, God put Abraham to the test. He said to him, "Abraham," and he answered "Here I am." And He said, "take your son, your favored one, Isaac, whom you love, and go to the land of Moriah, and offer him there as a burnt offering on one of the heights which I will point out to you."

Abraham dutifully takes Isaac to the place where he is to be sacrificed.

> Abraham built an altar there; he laid out the wood; he bound his son Isaac; he laid him on the altar, on top of the wood. And Abraham picked up the knife to slay his son. Then an angel of the Lord called to him from heaven: "Abraham! Abraham!" And he answered, "Here I am." And he said, "Do not raise your hand against the boy, or do anything to him. For now I know that you fear God, since you have not withheld your son, your favored one, from

Me." When Abraham looked up, his eye fell upon a ram, caught in the thicket by its horns. So Abraham went and took the ram and offered it up as a burnt offering in place of his son.

What this story tells us, if we read it metaphorically (and perhaps my hypothesis stretches things a bit) is that the association between the Jews and laughter is an important part of the earliest history of the Jews. Laughter is not to be killed, but maintained. Abraham is not to sacrifice "laughter" but preserve it, and so he sacrifices a ram, the first "stand in," providentially caught in a thicket, instead.

MORE SPECULATIONS ON JEWISH HUMOR

Let me return to the question of what is distinctive, if anything, about Jewish humor. We must keep in mind that there are some scholars who believe that there is no such thing as Jewish humor and, by implication, one would imagine, no ethnic humor of any kind. There is just humor. Personally speaking, I find this notion highly suspect.

There are, it seems to me, four basic categories as far as Jews, non-Jews, and Jewish jokes are concerned.

1. Jokes by Jews about Jews and other Jews
2. Jokes by Jews about Jews and non-Jews
3. Jokes by non-Jews about Jews and other Jews
4. Jokes by non-Jews about Jews and non-Jews

If we wish to talk about humor in general, we can add two more categories:

5. Jokes by Jews about non-Jews
6. Jokes by non-Jews about non-Jews

It seems pretty obvious to me that the first two categories are found in Jewish humor. The third and fourth categories, while they deal with Jews, are not Jewish humor; they may (and often do) attack and ridicule Jews.

The interesting question is number 5. Can a Jew tell a joke about non-Jews that qualifies as a Jewish joke? According to Avner Ziv's definition, the answer is no. Jewish humor must be created by Jews and deal with Jewish life. But if the joke reflects a Jewish sensibility, might such a joke not be Jewish? Number six, humor by non-Jews about non-Jews is, at first sight, categorically non-Jewish. But is it possible that, because of the "Yiddishization" of much American humor and culture, many non-Jews tell jokes about other non-Jews that are, in essence, Jewish jokes? That is, they reflect a Jewish sensibility—assuming such a thing exists.

If this "Yiddishization" phenomenon is true, categories three through six could generate some Jewish jokes. Is it conceivable—and this would be the height of irony—that Jew-hating non-Jews tell anti-Semitic jokes reflecting (unconsciously) a Jewish sensibility? And if an anti-Semitic Jew or self-hating Jew tells an anti-Semitic joke, is that Jewish humor?

There are, we can see, dilemmas that are created when we try to figure out what is and isn't a Jewish joke. To simplify matters, I will stick with the first two categories: (1) jokes that Jews tell about relationships between Jews and other Jews and (2) jokes that Jews tell about the relationships that exist between Jews and non-Jews.

A PSYCHOANALYTIC EXPLANATION: WHY THE JEWS ARE SUCH A COMIC PEOPLE

Earlier, I used the Torah to show the intimate relationship that exists between laughter, as personified by Isaac, and the first Jews—Abraham and Sarah. (This relationship is, I would suggest, part of the Jewish heritage and has influenced the development of Jewish culture and traditions.) Now I will turn to other explanations.

One reason Jews have developed such a remarkable sense of humor is that they have suffered so greatly. The Holocaust lingers in the background, reminding Jews that they never can be secure, and many Jews experience discrimination and anti-Semitism. Jews use humor, then, as a means of escaping from the pain they feel and have felt (collectively speaking) and from individual feelings of marginality. Jews use humor, in addition, to ward off the anxiety they feel about the future and deal with their feelings of hostility and anger in a way that enables them to express these feelings and avoid being punished for them.

There is, in much Jewish humor, a kind of existential courage as weak and powerless Jews contend, using humor, with people who discriminate against them, hate them, persecute them, and at times, kill them. Because of their marginality and relative weakness, Jews have used humor as a survival mechanism—not only to soothe their psyches but also to ensure, to the extent possible, that the societies in which they found themselves were democratic ones where they had a chance of being justly treated.

Anthropologist Gregor Benton has suggested, as a matter of fact, that the Jewish joke is actually the source of political jokes. Jewish jokes, he adds, provided consolation and the courage to survive—not only for Jews but for many people. As he explains in his essay "The Origins of the Political Joke" (in Chris Powell and George E.C. Paton's *Humour in Society: Resistance and Control*, 1988, 42,43):

> The Jewish joke as we now know it first developed in various national forms in nineteenth-century Europe during the movement for Jewish emancipation. It was renowned for its sarcasm and merciless irony, and also for its unique strain of self-irony. Paul Landau, writing in the early thirties, spoke of its "passionate hatred for all falseness and hypocrisy." The Jewish joke has been analyzed as a product of the acute self-consciousness and self-doubt of Jews who strove unsuccessfully to remake their personalities in ways acceptable to the broader community, and who ended up making enemies in both the community they were trying to leave and the one they were trying to enter. But, for Jews, even questions of cultural identity were directly political in those days. Jews in Eastern Europe and Tsarist Russia were harried whichever way they turned by racial bigots in the majority community and in the state bureaucracy. They stood outside *goyish* society, but were unable to avoid contact with it. It is not surprising that they developed a strong tradition of social and political criticism. This tradition found its expression partly in humour, and it is to the Jews that the world owes the first modern political joke.

Benton points out that Jewish jokes were widely popular in Central Europe as early as the middle of the nineteenth century, and by the end of the nineteenth century, collections of Jewish jokes were popular with non-Jews in cities such as Vienna and Berlin.

If the Jewish joke is secularized and the humor is directed at political institutions rather than the bizarre aspects of one's own community, for example, you get the political joke. It is not much of a leap, we can see, from the Jewish joke to the political joke. As we might expect, many Jewish jokes, especially contemporary ones, are political.

We can see this in an amusing joke that is based on the way many Jews use language.

The Trotsky Telegram

Stalin is standing on Lenin's mausoleum in Red Square. "Comrades," he tells the crowd. "An historic event has occurred! I have received a telegram of congratulations from Leon Trotsky!" The crowd hushes. Stalin reads: "Joseph Stalin. The Kremlin. Moscow. You were right and I was wrong. You are the true heir of Lenin. I should apologize. Leon Trotsky." The crowd roars. But in the front row a little Jewish tailor gestures to Stalin. Stalin leans over to hear what the tailor has to say. "Such a message," says the tailor. "But you didn't read it with the correct feeling." Stalin raises his hand and stills the crowd. "Comrades," he says, "we have here a simple worker who says I read Trotsky's message without the right feeling. I am asking the worker to read it to us the way he thinks it should be read." He gives the telegram to the tailor, who gets up to read the telegram. He clears his throat and reads: "Joseph Stalin. The Kremlin. Moscow. "You were *right* and *I* was *wrong? You* are *the true heir of Lenin? I* should *apologize?"*

It is the way the Jewish tailor reads the passage, with a Jewish inflection, that is so funny—as he takes a message and by reading it his way, turns its meaning completely around.

This joke only works if you understand the way some Jews talk and the way they stress words differently than other people. We have here not a Jewish accent, but a Jewish way of stressing words and speaking. This intonational pattern probably stems from the way Jews cantillate when they recite their prayers.

As Jacob L. Ornstein-Galicia explains in "Dem Kibbitzers Maven: Yiddish Language Contact and Affective Borrowing" (unpublished and undated paper), there are two types of phonological loans in Jewish jokes:

> a) adoption of the /sh/+ consonant cluster which comes from favorite borrowings like *shlemiel*, *shlimazel*, which can commonly be heard used by the female stars on the shows *Laverne and Shirley* and *Rhoda*, for example "shmuck," and "shnook," and others. A favorite pattern of use is in mocking or a derisive effect with the /sh/ pattern:
> Ex: "money, shmoney, what does it matter? . . ."

> b) More subtle than the segmental loan mention is the adoption of several intonational patterns which in their turn appear to have originated through the cantillation or reciting of Hebrew prayers. At any rate, the pattern most common is one that consists of a series of rises, punctuated by mild descending tone and ending with an interrogative upward tone of about level four:

                                                                 4. *art?*
                            3 *that's*
        2 *And you're*   2 *a work of*
              1 *telling me*

It is this pattern, in a minor variation, that we find in the joke about Stalin and the tailor. It is the variant stressing of "right," "wrong," "you" and "I" by the tailor that makes the difference and reverses the meaning of the passage. This pattern is an important one, as is the practice of placing a direct or indirect object at the start of a sentence, as in, "From *this* he's making a living?"

Benton suggests, in his conclusion, that the political joke has no lasting impact. As he writes (1988, 54):

> But the political joke will change nothing. It is the relentless enemy of greed, injustice, cruelty and oppression—but it could never do without them. It is not a form of active resistance. It reflects no political programme. It will mobilize no one. Like the Jewish joke in its time, it is important for keeping society sane and stable. It cushions the blows of cruel governments and creates sweet illusions of revenge. It has the virtue of momentarily freeing the lives of millions from tensions and frustrations to which even the best organized political opposition can promise only long-term solutions; but its impact is as fleeting as the laughter it produces.

I'm not as sure as Benton that Jewish jokes, political jokes, or any kind of jokes have no lasting significance.

It seems to me that jokes, by exposing bureaucratic ineptitude and political stupidity (as well as terror), can deprive a regime of any semblance of legitimacy and make a population much more receptive to change, revolution, what you will. Jewish jokes and political jokes are, in reality, forms of political, social, and cultural resistance, and their impact often lingers, I would suggest, long after the laugh.

POLITICAL CULTURES AND JEWISH JOKES

Aaron Wildavsky, who taught political science at the University of California at Berkeley before his untimely death, wrote that all democratic societies have four political cultures in them. He explained that membership in a political culture more or less shaped the political decision making and, by extension, the choice of films, television programs, songs and, one might add, jokes of individuals in each of the political cultures. I collaborated with Wildavsky on an article on humor and political cultures, and will be using some of the ideas and jokes in our essay in the material that follows.

As he wrote in his essay, "Conditions for Pluralist Democracy or Pluralism Means More than One Political Culture in a Country" (Survey Research Center, University of California, Berkeley):

> The dimensions of cultural theory are based on answers to two questions: "Who am I?" and "How Should I Behave?" The question of identity may be answered by saying that individuals belong to a strong group, a collective that makes decisions binding on all members or that their ties to others are weak in that their choices bind only themselves. The question of action is answered by responding that the individual is subject to many or few prescriptions, a free spirit or one that is tightly constrained. (Quoted in A. A. Berger, 1990, 5.)

According to Wildavsky, "there are only a limited number of cultures that between them categorize most human relations." He identified four political cultures: Fatalists, Individualists, Hierarchical Elitists, and Egalitarians (he changed the terms he used over the years).

He explained how these four groups can be elicited from the questions he asked about group boundaries being strong or weak and rules and prescriptions being numerous or few. As he put it:

> Strong groups with numerous prescriptions that vary with social roles combine to form hierarchical collectivism. Strong groups whose members follow few prescriptions form an egalitarian culture. Competitive individualism joins few prescriptions with weak boundaries, thereby encouraging ever new combinations. When groups are weak and prescriptions strong, so that decisions are made for them by people on the outside, the controlled culture is fatalistic. (Quoted in A. A. Berger, 1990, 6)

There are then four political cultures, each of which has different values and beliefs, different approaches to risk, different notions about ostentation, and so on. Members of each of these political cultures, if logic is followed, should like jokes that reinforce the values they believe in and shouldn't like jokes that attack their values. I am assuming here that people wish to avoid dissonance—ideas that conflict with their basic beliefs and values—and seek reinforcement—ideas that support their basic beliefs and values.

We can take a Jewish joke, then, and consider which political culture would be most likely to find it funny.

The World's Richest Synagogue
The scene is set in the world's richest synagogue, and the protagonists are the world's best rabbi and the world's finest cantor, as well as the shammas, the non-Jew who looks after the synagogue. After the

glorious Yom Kippur service, the three gather in the rabbi's office. The rabbi in the world's richest synagogue says to the world's best cantor that he has sung the Kol Nidre better than it has ever been sung before. In all modesty, the greatest cantor in the world says that his singing wasn't bad, but when he thinks of the great cantors of the past, he is really nothing. Then the cantor turns to the rabbi and says, "But rabbi, your sermon was the best that has been delivered anywhere at any time." In all due modesty, the world's greatest rabbi in the world's richest synagogue says that the sermon wasn't bad, but when he thinks of the great rabbis and great sermons of the past, he is really nothing. By this time the shammas thinks he understands how these Jews talk to each other and is determined not to be outdone. So when the rabbi and the cantor praise the shammas for having prepared the synagogue for the holiday better than it has ever been prepared before, the shammas replies, "The synagogue was prepared all right, but when I think of the great shammases of the past, I'm really nothing." At this point, in unison, the world's greatest rabbi and the world's greatest cantor in the world's richest synagogue turn to each other and say, "Look who says he's nothing!"

We can see that the *arriviste* shammas is being put down for aspiring to a status to which the rabbi and cantor believe he is not entitled.

This joke is not an egalitarian one, because it is the shammas, lowest person in the social order of the synagogue, who is being put down. It is also not an individualist joke, since the shammas is not able to rise in status, however good his work. It is not a fatalistic joke, because the shammas is an activist and tries. It is most obviously a hierarchical elitist joke in which those, whether individualist or egalitarian, who try to climb the ladder of status by mimicking the manners of those above them are doomed to failure.

Since the synagogue in this joke is the world's richest synagogue and the cantor is the world's greatest cantor and the rabbi is the world's best rabbi, we know that we are dealing with hierarchy and stratification and the joke appeals to hierarchical elitists. Thus, the ironic punch line, "look who says he's nothing!" reinforces the point. The rabbi and cantor are able to *say* that they are nothing because they *know* that they are the world's greatest, but the shammas is not entitled to this false modesty.

We can see, then, that jokes, even if they don't deal specifically with politics, often reflect values, attitudes, and beliefs that enable us to classify them as appealing most to one of the four political cultures. Since the Jews tend to be critics of societàl injustice, because they have a big stake in maintaining democratic institutions in societies, I would suggest that Jewish jokes, in general, tend to be egalitarian ones. Let me offer an egalitarian Jewish joke.

Yankeleh's Ploy
A famous rabbi was being driven by coach throughout Poland. At each stop, the rabbi would answer questions about the Torah. His coachman, Yankeleh, observed him carefully at each stop. One day Yankeleh said to the rabbi, "what would happen if

we switched positions and you drove me into the next town and I pretended to be the rabbi?" The rabbi laughed at Yankeleh's suggestion, for Yankeleh, not being a scholar, knew very little about the Torah. But he decided to humor Yankeleh, and so just before they reached the next town, the rabbi took the reins and Yankeleh went inside the coach and pretended to be the rabbi. When they reached the center of the town, the coach stopped and people gathered around. One of the sages from the town said to Yankeleh, for they thought he was the rabbi, "Rabbi, what does it mean in the Torah when it says . . ." and then he proceeded to say what it says in the Torah. "Ha," said Yankeleh, "that question is so easy I'll have my coachman answer it!"

In this joke, Yankeleh is shown to be a very shrewd individual, and though he does not possess a scholarly knowledge of the Torah, he has enough wit to get the rabbi to answer the question. This joke, I would suggest, has an egalitarian ethos to it.

George Orwell has written that every joke is a "tiny revolution." That isn't always true, since there are jokes that, as we have just seen in the synagogue joke, reinforce the status quo and appeal to hierarchical elitists. But many, if not most, Jewish jokes would serve gallantly and subtly as instruments of revolutions, even if only tiny ones.

3

On the Techniques of Jewish Jokes

Jewish jokes and Jewish humor in general, especially in the Old World, in which Jews were continually persecuted, are often described as the humor of the marginal, the weak, and the powerless. It is important that we keep this social and political situation in mind when we think about the important functions this humor served.

FUNCTIONS OF JEWISH HUMOR

First, Jewish jokes (and I will use the jokes as representative of Jewish humor in general, even though this may be stretching things a bit) enabled the Jews to hide their hostility, to mask their aggression, and thus have the comfort of their aggression and be saved from having to pay for it. This is because many of these jokes used indirection and ambiguity. Non-Jews (goys) who didn't understand (or couldn't "decode," to use the language of literary theory and semiotics) some of the references or allusions and didn't interpret the jokes the way they could be interpreted were blind to the point many of these jokes made.

Victor Raskin, in his *Semantic Mechanisms of Humor*, offers a concept he calls *scripts* that is useful here. He writes (1985, 81):

> The script is a large chunk of semantic information surrounding the word or evoked by it. The script is a cognitive structure internalized by the native speaker and it represents the native speaker's knowledge of a small part of the world. Every speaker has internalized rather a large repertoire of scripts of "common sense" which represent his/her knowledge of certain routines, basic situations, etc. For instance, the knowledge of what people do in certain situations, how they do it, in what order, etc. Beyond the scripts of common sense, every native speaker may, and usually does, have individual scripts determined by his/her individual background and subjective experience and restricted scripts which the speaker shares with a certain group, e.g. family, neighbors, colleagues, etc. but not with the whole speech community of native speakers of the same language.

These scripts, which are sometimes also called schemas or frames, provide people with a set of understandings that are necessary to make sense of many jokes. Non-Jews don't understand, in many cases, references and allusions found in Jewish jokes, so they don't really get the joke.

We can think of Jewish jokes as "figures" that make sense against the "ground" of Jewish religion, history, language, and culture. To understand Jewish jokes, in addition to being able to understand Yiddish (which isn't used in all Jewish jokes by any means), you have to know something about Jewish religion or Jewish social practices. If we divide Jewish jokes into Old World jokes that deal with the world of the shtetl and New World jokes that deal with the world of the suburbs, we find two different sets of knowledge are required. Let me suggest some of the topics one must know something about to understand these two kinds of Jewish jokes.

Old World Jokes	**New World Jokes**
Nineteenth Century	Twentieth Century
Rabbis	Orthodox Jews
Shuls	Conservative Jews
Yeshivas	Reform Jews
Schnorrers	Congregational Politics
Schlemiels	Rabbis
Schlamatzls	Jewish Mothers
Shadkens	Jewish American Princesses
Melameds	Country Clubs
Peasants	Doctors/Lawyers/Accountants
Yiddish language	Suburban Life
Marginality	Marginality
Anti-Semitism overt	Anti-Semitism often hidden

These two worlds are not mutually exclusive, of course. There are plenty of schlemiels and schlimazels in American Jewish jokes (and Jewish humor in general); both Old World and New World Jews have experienced growing up as a marginal ethnic group; and many New World Jews have experienced anti-Semitism, just like the Old World Jews. But there are differences, as well, as many of the jokes reveal.

Stereotypes play an important role in ethnic humor. They are group-held generalizations about members of other groups that are used to explain their behavior: Jews are cheap, Poles are dumb, Italians are cowards, and so on. Stereotypes need not be negative; indeed, some are positive and others are neutral. But generally speaking, stereotypes are negative and are used by people to legitimate their prejudices. (Technically, a stereotype is an example of synecdoche, in which a part is used to stand for the whole, or vice versa.) Stereotypes are an important component of much ethnic humor, as Christie Davies has pointed out in his book *Ethnic Humour Around the World*.

In addition to making allusions and references to matters that non-Jews wouldn't understand, Jews often mocked themselves and turned their aggression against themselves in what is often thought of as "victim" humor. This was used to put off attackers, to show that the Jews didn't need others to point out their foibles. They could do the job very well themselves, in part because they understood the nature of human frailty.

But this victim humor should not be looked upon as a technique through which the Jews accepted and internalized the hatred that racist and anti-Semitic elements felt toward them. It was not a case of prisoners accepting the values of their warders but just the opposite, I would suggest—a tactic of resistance in the face of overwhelming odds in hostile environments.

This matter of surviving in hostile environments explains the following joke, which is told in most books of Jewish jokes.

> ***Don't Cause Trouble***
> *Three Jews were going to be executed. They were lined up in front of a firing squad and the sergeant in charge of the firing squad asked each Jew whether he wanted a blindfold or not. "Do you want a blindfold?" he asked the first Jew. "Yes," said the Jew in a resigned tone. "Do you want a blindfold?" he asked the second Jew. "Okay," said the second Jew. "Do you want a blindfold?" he asked the third Jew. "No," said the third Jew. At this, the second Jew leaned over to the third one and said "Take a blindfold. Don't make trouble."*

The Jews in Eastern European shtetls (and elsewhere) had to figure out ways to survive in hostile environments, and one way to do this was to avoid the limelight, to not "make trouble."

ANTI-NEGRO JOKES AND TRIUMPHANT VICTIMS

Jews are not the only ones who use so-called victim humor to disarm their opponents; we find the same thing in the humor of American Blacks. In an article, "The Psychological Meaning of Anti-Negro Jokes" (*Fact*, March-April, 1964), D. J. Bennett tells the following joke, which I have slightly modified:

> ***The Redneck in New York***
> *A Southern redneck goes into a bar with an alligator on a leash. The man sits on a stool and the alligator sits on the stool next to him. The redneck asks the bartender, "Do you serve niggers?" "This is New York," said the bartender. "We serve Negroes!"*

"Good," says the southerner. "I'll have a Scotch . . . and give my alligator a Negro."

In his version of the joke, Bennett makes the punch line "Give my alligator a nigger." I don't think that's as strong a punch line as "Give my alligator a Negro," since the bartender has made a point of calling black people Negroes. (This article was written in 1964, when the term "Negro" was considered the correct word for black people.)

Bennett points out that stereotypes have to have some semblance of truth to be useful, but this "truth" is often imposed on a minority by the majority. As he writes (1964, 56)

> To be credible, the stereotype must contain some truth (which, like all half-truths, is the greatest lie). Ironically, the cultural weaknesses that are exaggerated and generalized in the stereotyped jokes are the direct result of ill-treatment by the dominant group. Fagin is a product of a gentile world which made it illegal for Jews to own land or go into the professions, Steppen Fetchit is a product of a white world that did not allow the Negro an education, and the "drunken, lazy" Indian is a graduate of the reservation. By harping on these weaknesses in our jokes, we reassure ourselves of our cultural, social, moral, and spiritual superiority. This is why race and nationality jokes are by far the most popular among the "better" members of the ridiculed group. No one feels the need to be superior to the thickly accented "ghetto" Jew more than the emancipated Jewish bourgeois, and nobody feels the need to separate himself from the ignorant, backward drawling Southern Negro more than the educated middle-class Negro.

Bennett quotes figures from an article in the *American Sociological Review* that show that the percentage of anti-Negro jokes in a Southern white university was 6.8 percent, while at a Negro university it was 15.8 percent.

Bennett admits that while he wasn't surprised to find that Southern whites liked sadistic anti-Negro jokes, he was surprised to discover that Negroes liked them as well. He explains this by suggesting that there is a masochistic element in the Negro's enjoyment of these jokes. Since it was inevitable that they must suffer, Southern Negroes learned to enjoy what they had to endure.

I would offer a slightly different interpretation of what the popularity of these anti-Negro jokes means for Negroes—or to use the modern term, African-Americans. I don't believe it represents masochism or that masochism involves learning to enjoy inevitable pain and suffering.

The African-Americans who told this joke were making fun of themselves and in so doing immunizing themselves, so to speak, from racist humor by bigots, racists, and so on. "There's nothing you can say about us," this joke says to racists, "that we've not already said about ourselves. We know our weaknesses, and that is one of our strengths." There is a kind of inoculation effect involved here.

I don't imagine that anyone hearing this joke would suggest that African-Americans are masochists who have internalized the hatred they sense around them and often experience into a masochistic self-hatred. I say this because Jews, who use victim humor, are often accused of being masochistic. I would argue that victim humor is generally not based on masochism or a sense of inferiority but just the opposite: a sense of superiority. "We can do a better job of insulting ourselves than you can" is, I suggest, the subtext in these jokes and in most of the victim jokes that members of ethnic groups tell about themselves. I will have more to say on this subject later.

There is also an element of sophisticated connoisseurship about people laughing at jokes that insult their ethnic or racial group. Many of these jokes are, from a technical viewpoint, funny—even if they are ugly and can lead to negative self-images. Being able to laugh at these jokes shows one has somehow transcended the stereotyping. If you can laugh at yourself, you've won the game and immunized yourself from laughter others direct at you.

Since we're dealing with anti-Negro jokes, let me offer a couple more that are widely known.

The Negro from Harvard
A young Harvard Negro, dressed in a Brooks Brothers suit and carrying several books in French, enters a bus in Manhattan and sits down next to a Southern lady. She becomes furious. Unable to contain herself, she stands up and shouts "Nigger! Nigger! Nigger!" The young Harvard Negro leaps up in fright: "Where? Where? Where?"

This joke reflects the desire many educated middle-class Negroes have to leave their racial identities behind and somehow merge with the white community, becoming what used to be described as Oreo Cookies: black on the outside, white on the inside. We find this assimilation tendency in many Jews, as well. Indeed, one of the purposes of Jewish jokes, I would suggest, is to help maintain boundaries, separating Jews from non-Jews.

Let me offer one more joke about Blacks that I find most amusing.

The Ugly Thing
A big Black man, with a brilliantly colored parrot on his head, went into a bar. "I'll have a beer," he said. The barkeeper asked, "Where did you get such a funny looking thing?" "In Africa," replied the parrot. "There are millions of them there."

Bennett offers another bit of humor that is quite interesting. He describes a cartoon that appeared in *The People's Voice of New York* after the riots in Detroit. The cartoon showed the following scene:

The Trophy
Two little boys are looking at some hunting trophies in the den of one of the boys' fathers. One of the boys points to one of the trophies mounted on the wall, which is the head of a Negro. He says to the other boy, proudly, "Dad got that one in Detroit last week!"

Many whites, Bennett said, didn't find the cartoon funny at all, while many Negroes thought it was very funny. The reason the whites didn't find the cartoon funny was because of the overt hostility and aggression reflected in the cartoon: Negroes are turned into "game," just like lions, tigers, and buffalo. The black people, on the other hand, recognized the aggression but also found it amusing that someone would be able to joke about them that way.

There is a "play frame" here that we must take into consideration. Cartoons, jokes, and other humorous texts have a somewhat different reality and are interpreted differently than insults and other forms of aggression not separated by a play frame.

USING THE FORTY-FIVE TECHNIQUES TO ANALYZE A JOKE

Let us move from a rather general and somewhat theoretical discussion of jokes and stereotypes to something much more specific, namely the techniques of humor we tend to find in Jewish jokes. In an earlier chapter, I listed the forty-five techniques of humor that I argue are found in all humor, and suggested that different styles of humor are formed by using certain constellations of techniques. In the chart below, I list the forty-five techniques alphabetically and number each technique.

1. Absurdity
2. Accident
3. Allusion
4. Analogy
5. Before/After
6. Bombast
7. Burlesque
8. Caricature
9. Catalog
10. Chase Scene
11. Coincidence
12. Comparison
13. Definition
14. Disappointment
15. Eccentricity
16. Embarrassment
17. Exaggeration
18. Exposure
19. Facetiousness
20. Grotesque
21. Ignorance
22. Imitation
23. Impersonation
24. Infantilism
25. Insults
26. Irony
27. Literalness
28. Mimicry
29. Mistakes
30. Misunderstanding
31. Parody
32. Puns
33. Repartee
34. Repetition
35. Reversal
36. Ridicule
37. Rigidity
38. Sarcasm
39. Satire
40. Scale, Size
41. Slapstick
42. Speed
43. Stereotypes
44. Theme/Variation
45. Unmasking

Figure 3.1. Techniques of Humor in Numerical and Alphabetical Order

I will use this typology to show the techniques operating in a typical joke, as a means of demonstrating that jokes are much more complex than we imagine they are. They often have a number of different techniques working together to generate the humor. (The analysis that follows is adapted from the introduction to my book *An Anatomy of Humor*, though it contains some modifications and some new material.)

The Tan

A man goes to Miami Beach for a vacation. After a few days there he looks in a mirror and notices he has a beautiful tan all over his body, with the exception of one area of his body—his penis. He decides to remedy the situation the next day so he'll have a perfect tan all over his body. So the next morning he gets up early, goes to a deserted section of the beach, takes off all his clothes and lies down. He starts putting sand over his body until only his penis remains exposed to the sun. A short while after he finishes covering himself with sand a couple of little old Jewish ladies happen to walk by. One notices the penis sticking out of the sand. She points it out to her friend. "When I was twenty, I was scared to death of them," she says. "When I was forty, I couldn't get enough of them. When I was sixty, I couldn't get one to come near me. . . . And now they're growing wild on the beach!"

The subject of this joke is human sexuality; we can tell that from the punch line, "And now they're growing wild on the beach." The fact that it takes place in Miami, which is where many Jewish people go for vacations, and has a couple of little old Jewish ladies in it is what gives it its Jewishness. It does not have many other Jewish markers in it, however.

What techniques are used in this joke, we may ask. First, I'd suggest we have number fifteen, eccentricity. The man's quest for a perfect tan, which leads him to cover himself over, except for his penis, makes the joke possible. The second technique is more problematical. I'd say it is number twenty-nine, mistakes. The old woman thinks, mistakenly, that now penises "are growing wild on the beach." It is not an example of ignorance; I use that term for people who are stupid, foolish, and so on. There is also the technique of exposure, number eighteen. When there is a comic frame, we find people exposing their genitals funny—perhaps because they are put into an extremely embarrassing situation and are violating the rule about not showing private parts in public places. In addition, there is the technique of repetition and pattern, number thirty-four, as the woman talks about how she felt about penises at twenty, at forty, and at sixty.

Thus, if we were to offer a formula for this joke based on its subject and techniques used, it would be:

SEX/15-29-18-34.

Reducing jokes to formulas is, of course, an exercise in absurdity, but it does have the value of demonstrating that jokes are often complex and make use of a number of different techniques in generating humor.

There are, I should point out, several good jokes that use the notion that all the jokes in the world are known and are numbered.

The Comedian Who Couldn't Tell Jokes

A convention of comedians is gathered together. Everyone knows all of the jokes in the world, which have been numbered. This saves comedians from having to tell the joke itself. One comedian gets up and yells "24,006." Nobody laughs. A comedian whispers to his friend, sitting next to him, "He never could tell a joke!"

The second joke involves the same situation.

The New Joke

A convention of comedians is gathered together. Everyone knows all of the jokes in the world, which have been numbered. This saves comedians from having to tell the joke itself. One comedian gets up and yells "266,452." Everyone laughs like crazy. A comedian whispers to his friend, "Never heard that one before."

I offer these jokes because they suggest the notion of reducing jokes to numbers is absurd and silly.

I do not tell jokes well, because I don't believe that telling jokes is the best way to be funny; it is better to use the forty-five techniques and create your own humor (which is not the same thing as creating your own jokes). I must admit, however, that when I tell the "tan" joke during lectures on humor or on other occasions, people generally find it extremely amusing. I have already dealt with the techniques found in the joke, or what makes it funny. I would like to offer some hypotheses that explain why it is funny, drawing upon the theories of humor mentioned earlier.

THEORISTS OF HUMOR AND THE TAN JOKE

From the point of view of superiority theorists, we laugh at this joke because we feel superior to various characters in this story. The man who feels he must cover every inch of his body with a tan at any cost (so to speak) is obviously very foolish, and the woman who thinks penises are growing wild on the beach is mistaken about the phenomenon she sees before her. The last sentence in the joke, "And now they are growing wild on the beach," is the punch line and can be taken, given our comic context, as an example of a mistake. The sentences preceding the punch line reveal a good deal about her sexuality and frustrations.

For the incongruity theorist, the absurdity of a man's penis sticking out of the sand instead of being between a man's legs, where it belongs (in the first place) and of a person thinking that penises can grow wild on the beach, like wild flowers (in the second place) is the source of the humor. One expects penises to behave and stay shielded from public scrutiny. The punch line generates the incongruity. It postulates penises growing like wild flowers or vegetables, dissociated from male bodies.

People's so-called private parts seldom get tanned as well as the rest of their bodies, and it is silly to want them to, just as it is incongruous to expose these private parts to the public. The joke, then, hinges on the incongruity of seeing private parts in public places.

To the psychoanalytic critic, the humor generated by the joke stems primarily from its sexual content. The humor in the joke is related to sexuality and the matter of sexual development in people and, in particular, to sexual hunger. The punch line represents a kind of wish-fulfillment, a sexually paradisical state for this old woman, where penises grow wild on the beach and are thus easily obtainable and in as great a quantity as may be desired. Sexual repression, which Freud postulated as being the price we pay for civilization, is no longer a dominating force. Penises grow wild on the beach and can be obtained (plucked) whenever you want one.

The man, it could be argued, also has unconscious exhibitionist tendencies that are masked by his alleged desire (fixation?) to obtain an even tan on every part of his body. There may also be a regressive aspect to the woman, who does not seem to know that penises always come attached to men—a means, a good Freudian might argue, of escaping from penis envy. Although this joke may be connected to psychological processes in individuals, it also has a very strong social component and refers to the problems related to stereotyped thinking about sexuality among the aged.

An analysis of this joke's logical structure shows something else. The punch line, "and now they're growing wild on the beach" sets up an binary opposition that contrasts the natural and the cultural. We can see this in the chart that follows:

Natural	*Cultural*
Growing Wild	Sexuality at twenty, forty, sixty
the beach	society
free sexuality	repression

It is this set of oppositions that gives us an insight into the real meaning of the joke, according to structural theorists: nature and culture are in conflict, and repression and sexual hunger are the consequences. Whether people recognize this at the conscious level is beside the point.

It is obvious that there are similarities between the psychoanalytic perspective—which argues that jokes (and works of humor in general) deal with unconscious phenomena such as drives—and the structural perspective—which suggests that people may not consciously be aware of the real meaning of jokes.

There is a political dimension to the tan joke that is worth considering. If we examine the joke, we find a number of attitudes or values reflected in it, all of which have political implications. For example, we find ridicule directed toward the man who lies naked on the beach and pours sand on himself until only his penis is showing. And we find ridicule directed toward the old woman (and by implication, the aged in general) who still has sexual desires but is frustrated. We often find humor connected with frustrating sexual impulses and activities in people and should not overlook the matter of power, here. The old frequently try (generally with little success) to control the sexuality of the young and dominate their sexual lives as well as other aspects of their lives.

There is also a political dimension to the ridiculing of the utopianism of the old woman. A society without repression, where penises grow wild on the beach and sexuality is free and uninhibited by social constraints, is, the joke suggests, absurd. There is, it could be argued, a conservative (hierarchical elitist?) impulse in this joke.

Contemporary feminist discourse often uses the term *phallocentric* to deal with society, the media and the arts, and the way they are dominated by men and male values. Could one find a more phallocentric text than the tan joke? In this joke, the women are frustrated sexually and not terribly intelligent, either. From a feminist perspective, this is an excellent example of the way males dominate females.

WHO'S RIGHT ABOUT THE TAN JOKE?

The logical question to ask is, who's right? The answer is, everyone, to a degree! That's because jokes don't have just one meaning; what you get out of a joke (or a film or a novel) depends on who you are, what you know, what you are like, and what you like. In a sense, we have one joke that becomes a number of different jokes, one for each perspective on humor and life. When it comes to humor, then, to take some liberties with street language, "there are different jokes (as well as different strokes) for different folks."

The formulaic analysis, I should point out, is not subject to the problems that "why" theories of humor cause. One problem with the "why" theories is that they tell you little about a specific joke. You always end up with a rather general statement: the humor in the joke is caused by superiority or by incongruity or something else. You don't get into much detail.

It is possible—with considerable precision, I would suggest—to determine the subject of a joke (though this isn't always the easiest thing to do) and the techniques used in the joke, in order of their importance. These techniques reveal to us how the joke, by using one or more techniques, generates humor, laughter, and mirth.

ON HUMOROUS TECHNIQUES AND POWER

Now that I have explained how my forty-five techniques of humor work and can be used to analyze or "deconstruct" a joke (or any kind of humor, for that matter), an interesting question suggests itself. Does the humor of those who are powerful tend to make use of certain techniques, and does the humor of those who are weak and marginal, like the Jews, make use of other techniques?

Let me offer a hypothesis that I will defend by citing some jokes. Those who are members of the majority, who belong to the dominant elements that have power in societies, use techniques of humor that tend to be direct and reflect their sense of superiority. Those who are relatively powerless, who are marginal, and who are often the victims of the humor of the powerful, use techniques that are indirect and ambiguous and whose meaning often escapes the notice or understanding of dominant elements.

I am not arguing that the powerful only use certain techniques and the powerless only use other techniques. There is a lot of overlapping, but the powerful tend to use some techniques and the weak tend to use others. The powerful, I would suggest, use techniques such as insult, stereotyping, ridicule, impersonation (my category for dialect humor), and definition. If you are a member of a dominant element in society, you don't have to mask your hostility as much as you do if you are a member of a weak and marginal group. I am assuming, of course, that all jokes are put into a play frame that tells the listener "this is not serious, but a kind of play." Insults, by themselves, are not humorous, and even in jokes they often are so overtly hostile that they aren't funny.

Members of dominant elements in a society use stereotyping as a means of making fun of ethnic, racial, sexual, and other minorities in society. They do this, as Christie Davies has pointed out, to escape from the burden (he cites Max Weber about the "iron cage") of rationality as well as to reinforce their feelings of dominance and superiority. Ridicule, which involves taunting, deriding, and mocking others, is also a technique much used by the powerful, though it is also used by the weak. Dialect—Jewish dialect, Southern "good old boy" dialect, Italian dialect, Japanese dialect, and so on—is often used by power elements. Some politicians use dialect in an attempt to be funny, generally with disastrous results. Senator Al D'Amato, a member of a much joked about ethnic minority himself, imitated a Japanese dialect while trying to ridicule Judge Lance Ito (who does not speak with a dialect) and received a great deal of negative publicity for doing so. The senator had to issue an apology. There are other techniques as well, such as definition, that could be mentioned, but I will not press the point.

Let me say something about techniques of humor that tend to be used by the marginal, the weak, and the relatively powerless. These techniques are more subtle and less obvious: irony, sarcasm, reversal, unmasking and revelation, wordplay and wit, absurdity, satire, eccentricity, allusions, repartee, mistakes, and imitation. I will also include stereotyping, because many Jewish jokes involve stereotypes—of Jews as well as of non-Jews.

I will offer a number of jokes in which the dominant technique comes from the list above. We must remember that we often find a number of different techniques at work in a joke—as "The Tan" joke shows—and it isn't always easy to determine which technique is the dominant one. Also, we must keep in mind that members of ethnic communities and other groups often enjoy telling jokes about themselves because they enjoy the cleverness and humor of the jokes, even if they are the victims of the jokes. With these caveats in mind, let us begin.

Irony

Irony, as I understand the term, refers to saying something and meaning the opposite of what you say. There are eiron figures, such as Socrates and various Jewish types we find in Jewish jokes, who pretend to ignorance but are really wise. And there are ironic situations, in which the opposite of what one desires comes to pass. In plays this is known as dramatic irony. The following joke is, I would suggest, an ironic one.

Yom Kippur
Three Jews are having an argument about how progressive their synagogues are. The first Jew says, "at Yom Kippur we provide ashtrays, so people can smoke during the services." The second Jew says, "That's nothing. We provide sandwiches during Yom Kippur—ham sandwiches." The third Jew smiles. "We beat that," he says. "During Yom Kippur we don't have services. We put up a big neon sign on the shul saying 'closed because of the Holy Days.'"

In this joke, Judaism is finished off. The shul doesn't have services on the holiest day in the Jewish religion; it is "closed for the Holy Days," which, in effect, says Judaism—at least the kind practiced by members of the progressive temple in the joke—is dead.

Here's another ironic joke.

A Name Change
A Jewish man named Katzman decided to change his name to something French, so people wouldn't

> know he was Jewish. He went to a judge for assistance. "French, you say," said the judge. "Let's see what we can do. The French word for cat is chat. And the French word for man is l'homme. So we'll change your name to Chat-l'homme."

Ironically, the man's name is changed to "Shalom," which is even more Jewish than Katzman is, in that it is widely recognized as being a Hebrew greeting. We also have, once again, the matter of Jewish identity dealt with, and the desire for assimilation. Katzman, we must remember, doesn't want people to know he's Jewish by his name.

Stereotypes

A stereotype, as I explained earlier, is a group-held oversimplified belief about members of some other group. Stereotypes are important because they provide a "ready-made," so to speak, understanding of the target group's behavior, motivation, attitudes, and so on. In *Ethnic Humor Around the World* (1990), Christie Davies suggests that ethnic jokes involve paired oppositions.

We can understand this if we consider the work of Ferdinand De Saussure, the Swiss linguist who explained in his *Course in General Linguistics* (1915), that "concepts are purely differential and defined not by their positive content but negatively by their relations with other terms of the system" (1966, 117). Meaning is determined not by content but by relations. The "most precise characteristic" of concepts "is in being what the others are not" (1966, 117).

I have elicited from *Ethnic Humor Around the World* a number of paired opposites, which are shown below:

Stupid	Canny (including sly, shrewd)
Dirty	Clean
Avaricious	Generous
Cowardly	Militaristic and brave
Egalitarian	Hierarchical
Lazy	Industrious
Crude	Sophisticated
In-Groups	Out-Groups

The first pair of opposites, stupid and canny, are, Christie suggests, "the dominant ethnic jokes of the modern world" (1990, 12).

With this in mind, let us consider two stereotyped figures in Jewish joke lore: the Jewish mother and the Jewish American Princess.

Home for Dinner

After being away for more than a year, a Jewish young man phones home from the airport.

"Hello, Ma, how are you?"

"Just fine, son. When are you coming home? I'll fix you some chopped liver, some chicken soup, and a nice pot roast."

"It'll take awhile. My flight just got in and I haven't got my luggage yet."

"I'm so excited. I'll make you your favorite dessert—some strudel."

"But I don't like strudel," says the young man.

"You don't?" says the woman.

"Say—is this Bigelow 4077?"
"No, it isn't! It's Bigelow 4076!"
"Then I've got the wrong number."
"Does that mean you're not coming?"

This joke deals with the stereotype of the Jewish mother who lives only, it seems, to feed her children. This is so much part of her role that when a person she thought was her son but is really a stranger calls by mistake, she wants to feed him. The punch line, "Does this mean you're not coming?" suggests that it is the stereotype of the Jewish mother that is the dominant technique in this joke. It is the mistake that makes the punch line possible.

The second stereotype is that of the JAP—the Jewish American Princess—a narcissistic, spoiled, and materialistic young Jewish woman who doesn't cook and doesn't want sex. JAP "jokes" are not really jokes, but riddles.

JAP JOKES (RIDDLES)

What does a JAP make most often for dinner?
Reservations.

What's an ideal house for a JAP?
5000 square feet, with no kitchen and no bedroom.

How does a JAP commit suicide?
She piles all her clothes on her bed, climbs to the top, and jumps off.

How many JAPs does it take to change a light bulb?
Two. One to get the diet cola and the other to call Daddy.

What's an incurable disease for a JAP?
Maids. She dies if she doesn't have one.

What's interesting about these two stereotypes is that they are polar opposites, as the following chart (taken from my *An Anatomy of Humor*) shows.

Jewish American Mother	*Jewish American Princess*
Has children	Avoids sex
Sacrifices for children	Self-centered existence
Cooks	Won't cook
Housewife role basic	Avoids housework
Overly concerned about children	Overly concerned about self
Scrimps and saves	Spends money freely
Jewishness basic	Americanness basic

The two figures come from different traditions: the Jewish American Mother is basically Old World Jewish, while the Jewish American Princess is essentially assimilated New World American. The figures are polar opposites: the Jewish mother cooks and wants to feed someone who calls her on the phone, even if he isn't her son and has dialed a wrong number, while the Jewish American Princess doesn't want to cook at all.

We must recognize, of course, that relatively few (and perhaps hardly any) young Jewish women are like the "Princesses" the jokes ridicule and that a number of young women who are not Jewish are like the "Princesses." In his article, "An Analysis of JAP-baiting humor on the college campus," in *Humor* magazine (1989, 2-4), Gary Spencer concludes that these jokes have very negative consequences. As he explains (1989, Vol. 2-4, 344):

We conclude from an analysis of our data that the JAP-baiting phenomenon is directed primarily at Jewish women and, as such, is both sexist and anti-Jewish. The content of the humor contains a stereotype of women that communicates a sense of place, appearance, and perceived moral failings. With moral failings identified, it is now permissible to move to sexual denigration and calls for physical violence and abuse. With the exception of graffiti, the entire activity is masked in a veil of humor that seems to legitimate the activity as harmless fun directed at women who are now perceived as deserving of the abuse.

These jokes help communicate prejudice, Spencer argues, and even legitimate acts of violence against young Jewish women. Thus, in his view, they are far from being harmless jests. Others, I should point out, have suggested that JAP jokes, though hostile, are not anti-Semitic and don't do as much harm as they are alleged to do.

Ignorance

Having stupid people do stupid things (the revelation of ignorance in people) is one of the most widely used techniques of humor, and comes in first in Christie's list of oppositions in ethnic jokes: stupid versus canny, sly, and shrewd. All kinds of jokes deal with stupid people and the stupid things they do, and stupid, inept, and zany people are found in elite literary works (stories, novels, plays) as well as in jokes.

In what I've described as Old World Jewish humor, there is a town called Chelm, where all the people are fools. Let me offer a few Chelm jokes.

The Lost Key
A man from Minsk is traveling and comes into Chelm. He notices a number of people are looking at the ground around a light pole. "What happened?" he asks. One of the townsfolk tells him, "Chaim lost his keys and we are looking for them." "I'll help you look," says the man. "He lost them around here, no doubt." "No," says the man from Chelm. "He lost them several blocks away—but the light here is better."

We see here an example of perverted logic. It makes sense to have light when you look for a lost key, but it is foolish to look for a key near a light post because the light is better there than at the place you lost your keys. But that is the point. The residents of Chelm are all fools.

The Buttered Bread Problem
Two sages from Chelm got into a philosophical argument. "Why is it," one said, "that whenever you drop a slice of buttered bread, it always lands on the buttered side?" "Is that true?" said the other sage. "Let's see." He took a piece of buttered bread and dropped it, but it landed on the side that wasn't buttered.

"Your theory doesn't work."

"Don't you know what you've done?" said the other sage. "You buttered the bread on the wrong side!"

We are very close to the theater of the absurd here, and these jokes from Chelm are similar to those found in plays by Ionesco, for example. We see this more clearly in my last Chelm joke.

The Question Of Growing

Two sages from Chelm were debating a question: At which end does a human being grow?

"What a silly question," said one sage. "It is obvious that people grow from the feet up."

"Give me some proof," said the second sage.

"I bought a pair of pants several years ago," says the first sage, "and they were so long that they trailed on the ground. Now, they're too short. That's my proof."

"You've got it wrong. It's just the opposite way," says the second sage. "It's obvious that we grow from our heads. The other day I saw a regiment of soldiers on parade, and I could see that at the bottom they were all the same; they differed in size only on the top."

This bit of nonsense is very similar to the question Ionesco raises in *The Bald Soprano*—why do newspapers give the age of deceased persons but not the age of the newly born?

There is a concept used in dramatic theory that is of interest here. Critics use the term *discrepant awareness* to deal with situations in which one or more characters in a play don't know some information that one or more other characters know, or that members of the audience know something that one or more characters don't know. That is, some characters in plays are ignorant of the fact, for example, that a male character is dressing up like a female character. When a male character becomes sexually attracted to a female character who is really a male, as in *Charley's Aunt*, all kinds of humorous consequences are possible.

In a sense, every joke involves ignorance and discrepant awareness on the part of the person or persons being told the joke—until the punch line—so there is something mildly ironic about our laughing at stupid characters and fools, since every joke is based on our being put into a position of ignorance, of discrepant awareness, ourselves.

Unmasking and Revelation

Unmasking and revelation involve situations in which we discover things about people, generally of an embarrassing nature, that they tried to keep hidden. In the following joke, we find an excellent example of the unmasking and revelation technique.

Minding My Own Business

A minister comes home early one day and finds his wife naked in bed and a strong smell of cigar smoke in the apartment. He looks out the window and sees a priest, smoking a big cigar, walking out of the house. In a rage, the minister takes the refrigerator and pushes it out the window, where it falls on the priest, killing him. In a fit of remorse, the minister jumps out the window and dies. Two seconds later, a priest, a minister, and a rabbi appear at the pearly gates before St. Peter. "How did you get here?" St. Peter asks the priest. "I was walking out of this apartment house and a refrigerator fell on me, killing me instantly," says the priest. "I pushed that refrigerator out a window, killing the priest. And in a fit of remorse, I jumped out the window, killing myself," says the minister. "And what about you?" St. Peter asks the rabbi. "I don't know how I got here," says the rabbi. "I was minding my own business, sitting in a refrigerator, smoking a cigar...."

The rabbi, obviously, was the one involved with the minister's wife, but the poor priest got blamed. Thus, when the rabbi says that he doesn't know how he got to the pearly gates, he's being a bit incredible and we realize that while he might have been minding his own business sitting in the refrigerator, he was up to monkey business earlier.

Absurdity

This joke is a famous one that deals with a common stereotype in Jewish jokes (and humor in general), the monster Jewish mother. I use the term absurdity here in a somewhat specialized way—dealing with logical problems and that kind of thing, rather than just crazy stuff. If you use the term absurdity loosely, just about everything funny can be seen as absurd.

The Two Ties
A Jewish mother brings her son two ties for his birthday. "Thanks, Mom," he says. "They're beautiful." He goes upstairs and puts on one of the ties. When he comes down, his mother looks at him and says, "What's the matter? You don't like the other tie?"

The "logical" problem the son faces here is that he is caught in a tragic dilemma: no matter what he does, he's made a mistake. He puts on one tie, to show his mother he likes the gift she gave him, and she responds by asking, in essence, why he's not wearing the other tie. If he wore the other tie, she'd ask him the same question. In other words, nothing he can do can satisfy her.

Let me offer another joke that involves a logical absurdity, a joke that Freud tells in his book on jokes.

Salmon and Mayonnaise

An impoverished individual named Goldberg borrows twenty-five florins from a prosperous friend Cohen, saying he needs the money to feed his starving family, etc. A short while later, Cohen sees him in a restaurant with a plate of salmon and mayonnaise in front of him. "What's going on here?" says Cohen. "You borrowed money from me saying you needed to feed your starving family and here you are, in a restaurant, eating the most expensive dish in the place. Is that *what you've used the money for?" "Look," says Goldberg. "If I don't have any money I* can't *eat salmon and mayonnaise, and if I have money, I* shouldn't *eat salmon and mayonnaise. So—when* am *I to eat salmon and mayonnaise?"*

As Freud points out, and I've modified his joke a bit here, Goldberg shifts the situation from one in which a poor man eats an expensive meal with money he has just borrowed to the logical problem of when Goldberg can eat salmon and mayonnaise. He can't eat salmon and mayonnaise when he has no money, and he shouldn't eat salmon and mayonnaise when he does have money (which he has borrowed). So when is he to eat salmon and mayonnaise, he asks.

Mistakes

A mistake is some kind of an error a person makes due to ignorance, inattention, or whatever. I distinguish mistakes from misinterpretation, which involves some kind of a communication problem. The following joke is a good example of a joke involving a mistake.

The Matzos

A man finishes his lunch and leaves a delicatessen. As he leaves, he notices a blind beggar standing in the doorway, holding his hand out. The man happens to have a couple of pieces of matzos, so he puts one of the matzos in the hand of the blind beggar. The beggar fingers the matzos for a few seconds and says, "This guy writes like shit!"

The humor in this joke involves the man "reading" the matzos as if it were Braille—that is, mistaking the matzos for a literary work—and announcing that the writing is terrible.

Repartee

Here is a short joke that is repeated in just about every book of Jewish jokes I've read.

The Jew and the Nazi
A Nazi sees a Jew walking toward him. As the Jew passes by, the Nazi says "Schwein." The Jew tips his hat and says "Cohen."

This is an excellent example of repartee, in which hostility that is directed towards one is returned, in spades. When the Nazi walked by Cohen and said "schwein," he called Cohen a swine, but when Cohen tipped his hat and announced his name, it had the effect of making the Nazi's statement an announcement of his name.

Misunderstanding

This technique is commonly used in jokes. I distinguish between a mistake, which is something we do, an error we make due to our ignorance or some other deficiency, and misunderstanding, which involves a failure to communicate clearly and effectively. The joke that follows is, in my opinion, based on a misunderstanding rather than a mistake. Mistakes are, in my typology, part of the humor of logic, while misunderstandings are part of the humor of language. There is no language per se in the joke that follows, but there is, one can argue, a kind of sign language involved. Often we find misunderstandings leading to mistakes, I should point out.

The Pope and the Rabbi
The Pope issues a Papal Bull announcing that the Jews are to be expelled from Rome. The Pope calls

in the Chief Rabbi of Rome, but he doesn't speak Italian and the Pope doesn't speak Yiddish, so the Pope decides to communicate with the Chief Rabbi by gestures. When the Chief Rabbi comes into his chamber, the Pope makes a circle in the air. The Rabbi points up to the ceiling with his middle finger. The Pope then holds up three fingers. The Rabbi holds up his index finger. The Pope takes an orange from his cassock. So the Rabbi pulls out a piece of matzos. As a result of this interchange, the Pope tears up the Papal Bull expelling the Jews. Later that day, the Pope explains to one of his cardinals why he tore up the bull. "I made a circle in the air to suggest that God is everywhere, but the Rabbi put a finger in the air that meant you are at the center. Then I raised my hand with three fingers, meaning that God is triune. The Rabbi raised one finger, meaning that God is also one. Finally, I took out an orange and held it in the palm of my hand to show that God holds the world in the palm of his hand. The Rabbi took out a piece of matzos to show that we all have common religious traditions. As a result of this, I tore up the bull."

The Chief Rabbi, when he got back to his congregation, explains what happened somewhat differently. "The Pope made a circle in the air, meaning we're surrounded. I stuck a finger in the air to say 'up yours!' Then he put three fingers in the air, which meant we had three days to leave Rome. I put a finger in the air meaning that three days, one day—we're not leaving. And then we took out our lunches."

In this joke, the Pope and the Chief Rabbi misinterpret what each other does, and the humor lies in the cleverness of the joke and the various misinterpretations that are made.

CONCLUSIONS

In this chapter I have suggested that it is possible to look at Jewish jokes in terms of their humorous techniques rather than their subject matter—that is, the ways they generate humor rather than the topic or topics they deal with. We can look at jokes from a number of perspectives:

1. the subject matter of the joke
2. the techniques used in the joke
3. the themes in the joke
4. the form of the joke (standard joke or riddle).

I am partial to focusing on techniques because of the problems of classifying jokes in other ways. Vladimir Propp, in his *The Morphology of the Folktale*, argued that he developed his typology of functions (what a character does relative to the action of the tale) because it was the only way he could find of making sense of the tales he was dealing with. All of the various classificatory schemes that others had worked out broke down and turned out to be useless.

I'm not saying that it is wrong to classify jokes according to subject matter, only that it is a good idea to look at jokes in other ways as well. These techniques show how jokes (and other comic texts as well) generate humor and laughter, and even though my typology might be inelegant, as some have described it, there is no other typology I know of that enables us to see how words generate humor with as much precision as my forty-five techniques do.

Because of the social marginality and relative political weakness of Jews in the Old World as well as the New World, they tend to use certain techniques—ones that they can "get away with," ones that are not too obvious, that do not ruffle feathers too much. America might be a special case because of the "yiddishization" of American humor by Jewish comedians and writers, but even in America, there is still a considerable amount of anti-Semitism that generates anxiety and unease in Jews.

4

Schlemiels, Schlimazels, and Other Jewish Fools and Comic Types (Old World and New World)

A look at Jewish jokes and Jewish folklore from Eastern Europe shows that the humor deals with a remarkable variety of comic types. There are schlemiels, schlimazels, schnorrers, shadkens, fools, nitwits, and other kinds of eccentric characters in the jokes and folk tales. In this chapter, I will deal with schlemiels, schlimazels, and a couple of other types, but before I do, I would like to say something about the various zanies found in Jewish jokes and folklore and explain why we find eccentrics and "types" funny.

ON JEWISH TYPES IN JOKES AND FOLKLORE

In *A Treasury of Jewish Folklore*, Nathan Ausubel explains why Jewish humor has so many different kinds of absurd characters. He writes (1978, 386):

... Though different, from one another, every type had an organized unity with the rest, because all emerged from the same social-cultural environment. The confined ghetto of bygone days, in which Jews led their own semi-autonomous existence, was an entertaining as well as a tragic microcosm.

The Jew ... found time to scoff as well as to revere, to be skeptical as well as to extol. This was not done from caprice or malice, but rather out of good-humored raillery, prompted by a recognition that the noblest and wisest also have their comic and foolish sides. Therefore, all life passed in review before the folk-humorist who was no respecter of persons or of the degree of their eminence. Everybody without exception was a candidate for the butt of his jokes: preachers and rabbis, scholars and teachers, sextons and charity collectors, cantors and marriage brokers, waiters and innkeepers ... philanthropists and misers. In short, it was the procession of the whole Jewish people, a motley array of characters in all of their complex laugh-provoking relationships.

We see, then, that there is an egalitarian ethos to Jewish humor: all are eligible to be made fun of, no matter what one's profession is or how wealthy or powerful he or she is.

That egalitarianism is an important factor of Jewish jokes, also, as we will see. The extreme tensions existing in the shtetl, what Ausubel describes as "volatility," also contributed in great measure to the need for humor as a relief mechanism, and the diffuse anxiety that many Jews feel in contemporary societies also helps explain the need for humor to make life tolerable if not more pleasurable.

ON THE HUMOR OF TYPES

In my typology of techniques, I have a number of entries that deal with comic types, either directly or indirectly: eccentricity, rigidity, and grotesques. Eccentrics, as I understand the term, are "code violators," people who don't follow the same rules and norms that most people do.

There is a popular saying in America—"If you're poor, you're crazy. If you're rich, you're eccentric." Eccentrics, I would argue, flourish in societies where there is a strong degree of stratification. In egalitarian societies, there is a great deal of pressure on individuals to conform to societal norms. In hierarchical societies, people are more or less free to go their own way, especially if they are from the elites. Recent studies indicate, interestingly enough, that eccentricity is growing in America, which might indicate that we are becoming a more hierarchical and elitist society.

Rigidity, as I use the term, involves people who are comic monomaniacs, who are so single-minded in their actions and behavior that they often outsmart themselves. I consider braggarts, buffoons, cowards, pedants, misers, and so on examples of rigid types, not necessarily eccentric types, though in some cases it may be hard to draw a line between them. The grotesque involves elements of eccentricity and rigidity in it, but also an element of terror mixed with the comic.

The philosopher Henri Bergson, who happened to be Jewish, had an explanation of why we find types comical. In his essay "Laughter," he describes laughter as being caused "by something mechanical encrusted on the living" (Sypher, 1956, 88). As Bergson explains: ". . . this view of the mechanical and the living dovetailed into each other makes us incline towards the vaguer image of *some rigidity or other* applied to the mobility of life, in an awkward attempt to follow its lines and counterfeit its suppleness." This leads him to suggest that individuals are comic if they go their own way (the way rigid people do) without concern for others; that is, they are unsociable rather than immoral (though some comic types are immoral as well, I would add); they are machinelike automatons who do not show the suppleness and resilience of human beings.

He then suggests how the mechanical and the living relationship leads to types of people who are invariably comic (Sypher, 1956, 156):

> In one sense it might be said that all *character* is comic, provided we mean by character the *ready-made* element in our personality, that mechanical element which resembles a piece of clockwork wound up once for all and capable of working automatically. It is, if you will, that which causes us to imitate ourselves. And it is also, for that very reason, that which enables others to imitate us. Every comic character is a *type*. Inversely, every resemblance to a type has something comic in it.

All comic characters are types, from Bergson's point of view, and all types are comic in that they are, by definition, monomaniacal, rigid, mechanical, fixated, and as such, objects of our laughter.

One of the things that always fascinated me about the jokes from the Old World was the sweetness and tolerance the people in the shtetls had for eccentrics and zanies that is reflected in this kind of Jewish humor. Despite the problems of poverty and oppression, and the harshness of life in the shtetls, there seemed to be an attitude of tolerance and acceptance for the remarkable collection of zanies mirrored in the Old World Jewish jokes and tales.

JEWISH DIALECT IN JEWISH JOKES

Stanley Brandes, in an article titled "Jewish-American Dialect Jokes and Jewish-American Identity" (*Jewish Social Studies*, Fall 1983), points out that in the 1950s, a rather large proportion of Jewish-American jokes used the Jewish dialect. As he explains (1983, 234):

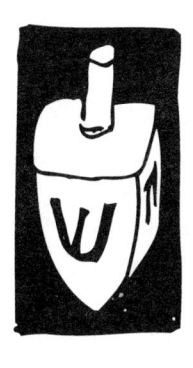

> What sets apart Jewish-American dialect jokes from most Jewish jokes told in prewar Europe, however, is that they recount a specifically linguistic story; they both reflect and demonstrate preoccupation with changing speech patterns over several generations in the New World. In fact, a survey carried out in 1950 determined that over a third of Jewish jokes in currency at that time utilized some form of dialect.

As a result of the education of second and third generation Jewish Americans and the forces of assimilation, this proportion must be lower today. A Jewish accent in the 1990s serves as a reminder of what once was, rather than a picture of what is—as far as dialect in the speech of Jewish Americans is concerned. These dialect jokes, Brandes argues, enable later generations of American Jews "vicariously" to have the same linguistic struggles that their parents and grandparents had.

Brandes tells an amusing joke about accents, which I have modified slightly:

Do You Speak Yiddish?
An old Jewish man in a theater taps a person sitting beside him on the shoulder and asks, "Do you speak Yiddish?"
"No," says the person.
He then taps a person sitting on the other side of him and asks, "Do you speak Yiddish?"
"No," says the person.
He then taps a person sitting in front of him on the shoulder and asks, "Do you speak Yiddish?"
"Yes," says the person.
"Vell, vot time is it?"

Brandes suggests that the humor in this joke is based on "the innocence of the man who subconsciously equates the Yiddish language with a Yiddish accent" (1983, 235).

In my typology, this joke would be described as one based on the mistake of the man assuming he was speaking Yiddish when he was just talking with a Jewish accent. In the background, we might note an element of anxiety here: maybe the Jewish man assumes people won't understand his accent if they don't speak Yiddish or, at the very least, are not Jews?

According to Brandes, Jewish-American jokes are not told by immigrants but are mostly told by second and third generation American Jews—a group of widely dispersed individuals, many of whom have little connection with Judaism and Jewish institutions, who want to assimilate into American culture and cast off, so to speak, their Jewish identities. Ironically, Brandes suggests in his conclusion, these jokes signify two contradictory phenomena. These dialect jokes, he suggests, stem from the insecurity that Jewish Americans have about their ethnic identities. As he writes (1983, 239):

> In a non-threatening, humorous vein, these anecdotes recount the linguistic tribulations, embarrassments, and triumphs of a people. They provide an emotional outlet and an informal sociological history. They are also tests and demonstrations of specialized knowledge, however, and thereby serve to reinforce ethnic unity. Paradoxically, Jewish dialect stories bear witness to the perpetuation of a tradition at the same time that they describe its demise.

It is a further irony, I would add, that as Yiddish terms become increasingly part of the American vocabulary, spread in large part by the media (many of the writers and performers in television and films are Jewish), the Jews' worst fears are coming true: the amount of intermarriage is extremely high, at around 50 percent nationally (and even higher in some areas, like the San Francisco Bay area). So more people are using Yiddish as there are fewer and fewer Jews, proportionally speaking.

In addition to borrowing a number of terms (listed and defined in the Glossary), Jewish jokes use a particular syntax, which I mentioned earlier. (What follows is based in good measure on Ornstein-Galicia's unpublished essay, "Dem Kibbitzers Maven: Yiddish Language Contact and Affective Borrowing.") This involves a syntax in which direct and indirect objects are placed at the beginning of sentences, as in "From this he's making a living?"

There is also the matter of the phonological loans I discussed earlier—the clustering of "sh" sounds plus consonants, as in the famous "Oedipus, Shmoedipus, as long as you love your mother" joke. And there is use of rises, as in the joke about Stalin reading a telegram from Trotsky. By changing the emphases, but not the words, the little Jewish tailor makes Trotsky's telegram mean just the opposite of what Stalin thought it meant.

Ornstein-Galicia cites two other important factors relative to telling Jewish jokes. The first is kinesics, the use of gestures or body language. As he points out:

> Although converging in large cities with kinemes [body movements] also common to other Mediterranean people such as Italians, non-Jewish New Yorkers and people in show-business have borrowed some typically Yiddish kinemes, such as, frequent brisk shoulder shrugging, flinging both hands outward and raising them while looking upward, forcing body contact, sometimes by pressing a finger into some part of the other person's body, standing spatially much looser than the Anglo-Saxon pattern considers proper.

I would add to this facial expressions. When you tell a Jewish joke, you must be expressive in addition to all the other things.

There is also the matter of the various rhetorical devices that are typically found in Yiddish, such as hyperbole, affirming something by the negation of its opposite (what rhetoricians call "litotes"), and minimization, among other things.

So in addition to using Yiddish terms, you have to use Jewish dialect (a good deal of the time, that is), intonation, gestures, and rhetorical patterns, if you are to tell—or perhaps it would be better to say perform, since there's so much involved—Jewish jokes correctly. At the end of his paper, Ornstein-Galicia offers an example of an Old World shtetl Jewish curse (which he got from Joe Singer's *How to Curse in Yiddish*) that also serves as a primer on Jewish food: "May you eat chopped liver with onion, pickled herring, chicken soup with matzo balls, carp with horseradish, boiled beef with tsimmis, potato pancakes with applesauce, tea with lemon every day and may you choke on every bite." These foods, incidentally, are still available (for the most part) in Jewish delicatessens and restaurants in urban areas where there are large numbers of Jews.

There is another function that dialect has in jokes: it establishes a play frame and tells the listener that what is being recounted is not "serious" but something humorous. William Fry, Jr., explains this in *Sweet Madness: A Study of Humor* (1968, 144): "Dialect is a common humor technique and, in one sense, it reemphasizes the 'this is unreal' quality of the episode. By definition, 'dialect' refers to a type of speech which is not the same as the speech of the joker. It is a type of speech which is, in this sense, unreal." So dialect helps establish the fact that a joke or something humorous is being told, and thus helps create the play frame that is necessary for the techniques of humor to be operative. Insults are not funny by themselves; it is only in a play frame, where we realize the insults are not really meant, and where other techniques are also at work, that insults amuse us. It is also helpful in telling jokes, Fry points out, for the joke teller to laugh from time to time and be amused by the joke he or she is telling, furthering or reinforcing the notion that something humorous is going on.

Now that we have discussed Bergson's theory of types, which explains why types are comic, the significance of dialect in establishing play frames, and the nature of Jewish dialect jokes, we are ready to look at some of the fools who inhabited the shtetls and who play such an important role in Old World Jewish humor. We will start with the schlemiel, one of the most important of the Jewish fool figures, who not only plays an important role in jokes and folklore but also is found in numerous American literary works with heroes who are, in essence, schlemiels.

THE SCHLEMIEL

First of all, we must recognize that the schlemiel is a fool. Ruth R. Wisse makes this point in her book *The Schlemiel as Modern Hero*. She explains (1971, 4): "The Jewish schlemiel is merely one version of the fool, 'a man who falls below the average human standard, but whose defects have been transformed into a source of delight.' The schlemiel shares many of the fool's characteristics and is used in many of the stock situations."

This notion of falling below standards is very close to Aristotle's definition of comedy as "an imitation of men worse than average," of men and women who are "ridiculous." This notion suggests that humor is based on feelings of superiority.

The schlemiel character is actually a somewhat complex and ambivalent symbolic figure. As Wisse writes (1971, 4,5):

> Though the Jewish fool began as a typical prankster and wit in the Middle Ages, his utility as a metaphor for European Jewry was later perceived by the folk and its formal writers. Vulnerable, ineffectual in his efforts at self-

advancement and self-preservation, he emerged as the archetypal Jew, especially in his capacity of potential victim. Since Jewry's attitudes towards its own frailty were complex and contradictory, the schlemiel was sometimes berated for his foolish weakness, and elsewhere exalted for his hard inner strength.

Reformers saw him as a symbol of weakness that had to be overcome, but other Jews saw him as a symbol of one who suffers through no fault of his own, but as the result of external conditions, and praised his innocence and his powers of endurance.

The basic attributes of the schlemiel, according to Leo Rosten in *The Joys of Yiddish*, are that he is a simpleton, he is unlucky, he's clumsy and gauche, he's a social misfit, he's naive and gullible, and he makes foolish bargains. Schlemiels, Rosten adds, are seen as pitiful characters, like *nebechs* and schlimazels. Nebechs are pitiful characters who are unlucky, but they have a special role in life—to clean up messes made by schlemiels. And schlimazels suffer from the clumsiness of schlemiels. Thus, a schlemiel will inevitably spill his soup on a schlimazel (a passive victim type of fool), and the nebbech will clean it up.

The function of fools like schlemiels, Wisse tells us, was to counter the heavy stress put on learning in the shtetls and other Jewish communities. As she writes (1971, 10): "Yiddish folk humor yielded up a limitless variety of fools, most of whom challenged not the political status quo or the prestige of the Biblical canon, but the heavy emphasis in the culture on learning, and the singular status of the scholar." This explains the importance of Chelm jokes about a community of fools who come up with absurd solutions to problems. The Chelm jokes, she tells us (1971, 11), "ridicule sophistry, or sterility of thought, which is dissociated from practical experience. Intellectualism is here turned on its head." The function of stories like those about Chelm, which poke fun at the arid intellectualism of the yeshivas, are to suggest that absurd interpretations of experience can lead to a sense of optimism while rational analyses inevitably lead to pessimism and despair.

There were, Wisse tells us, a remarkable collection of fools in the Yiddish folk repertory, such as (1971, 13):

> ... the *nar*, *tam*, *yold*, *tipesh*, *bulvan*, *shoyte*, *peysi*, *shmendrik*, *kuni lemel*, *shmenge*, *lekish*, and *lekish ber*, to name but a limited assortment. The schlemiel originally derived from a different category, the catalog of the luckless or inept, like the *schlimazel*, the *goylem, lemekh*, general terms, or more specifically, the *nisrof* (who was burned out), the *yored* (who had lost his fortune), the *onverer* (who had gone into bankruptcy), the *farshpiler* (who had lost his money gambling), or the *loy yutslakh*, the literal good-for-nothing.

Schlemiels were only one of a large number of different kinds of fools, each of which represented a particular kind of folly or ineptness. Schlemiels are (1971, 14) "active disseminators of bad luck," she adds, whose "misfortune is his character" and whose comedy is "existential."

Wisse offers an example of a joke about a schlemiel that raises the question as to whether schlemiels are always as foolish as they are supposed to be. This is a very common joke, I might point out, that is told in a variety of ways, with minor modifications.

The Battle
The Battle of Tannenberg was at its height when a czarist officer drew up his company and addressed them. "The moment has come! We're going to charge the enemy. It'll be man against man in hand combat." In the company was a Jewish soldier who was not fond of the czar or his war. "Please, sire, show me my man!" he cried. "Perhaps I can come to an understanding with him?"

In this joke, the Jewish soldier is a schlemiel figure who misinterprets what the czarist officer says and takes his "man to man" comment literally. He asks to be told which enemy soldier is *his* man, so he can reason with him and avoid bloodshed, violence, and so on. We see several important elements of Yiddish humor here. First, there is the misinterpretation, that overliteralness that is a hallmark of many fools. Second, we find the Jewish emphasis on rationality and logic and "coming to an understanding" as a means of solving problems, which is not what happens in military battles, where power and violence are the significant factors.

It is ironic, but perfectly understandable, that a society that focused so much energy on intellectual matters and esteemed scholars so highly (and the interpretation of the Torah, in particular) would generate, at the opposite pole, so many different kinds of fools. The fools provided a kind of equilibrium, I would suggest, and prevented people from pushing too far in any one direction.

Let me offer several other (and perhaps more representative) schlemiel jokes, in which the stupidity or ineptness of the schlemiel is shown more clearly.

The Boss
A Schlemiel was married to a really shrewish woman, who ordered him around all the time. Once, while the woman was entertaining some friends at tea, she decided to show her friends how much control she had over her husband.

"Schlemiel," she commanded. "Get under the table."

Her husband, without saying a word, got under the table.

"Schlemiel," she then said, "come on out!"

"No!" he said, angrily. "I'll show you and your friends who's master in this house!"

The schlemiel in this joke is typical of a subcategory of schlemiels—henpecked husbands.

The Absentminded Scholar
There was an absentminded scholar who was always losing things. One day he came back from a visit to the bathhouse without a shirt.

"Where's your shirt, schlemiel?" asked his wife. "Oh . . . my shirt. Someone must have exchanged his shirt for mine at the bathhouse."

"Then where is his? You don't have a shirt on," she replied.

"Tsk, tsk," reflected the scholar. "The man must have been terribly absentminded. He forgot to leave me his shirt."

These jokes are more representative of schlemiel jokes, with inept and weak characters, than the one about the Jewish soldier, whose stupidity has an element of wisdom about it.

THE SCHLIMAZEL

The term, Rosten points out, combines the German *schlimm* (bad) and the Hebrew *mazel* (luck) to describe a person who is always unlucky, a "born loser," someone for whom nothing turns out well. Rosten combines four folk sayings to describe this type of character (1963, 356):

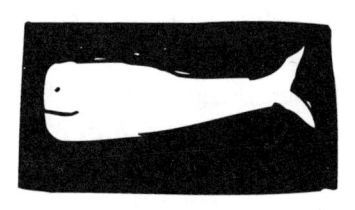

"When a *schlimazel* winds a clock, it stops; when he kills a chicken, it walks; when he sells umbrellas, the sun comes out; when he manufactures shrouds, people stop dying."

There is, then, something fated about the schlimazel, who exists, it seems, so the schlemiel can spill soup on him. Al Capp had a character in his comic strip *Li'l Abner* named Joe Btfsplk, who wandered around with a black cloud (a symbol of bad luck) hanging over him, symbolizing back luck for others; he turned others into schlimazels. I have also suggested in my book *Li'l Abner: A Study in American Satire* that the Shmoo (a modification of schmuck) figure in the strip was really a penis—a gag that Capp, who was Jewish, put over on the American public.

The following definitions of some of the terms used by Wisse are adapted from Leo Rosten's *The Joy of Yiddish*. I have also added a few more important terms. A *nar* is a fool or buffoon. A *yold* is a simpleton, a boob, a person whose stupidity and naiveté often get him into trouble. A *bulvan* is a brutish, insensitive, thick-skinned oaf. A *shmendrik* is a weak, thin, pip-squeak, a nobody, a person who thinks he can succeed, but can't. A *kuni lemmel* is what we would call a country bumpkin, a yokel. To this list we can add *shmeggeges*, *shmucks*, *schnorrers*, *shnuks*, *shloomps* and, forsaking the letter "s," *paskudnyaks*. A *shmeggege* is a maladroit, untalented petty person, a whiner and hot-air artist. A *shmuck* is a jerk or a son-of-a bitch. The term also means penis. A *schnorrer* is a beggar, a moocher, a compulsive bargain hunter, an indigent who is impudent and feels he has a right to be fed and given money. There is also the element of bum and drifter that is often attached to the term. A *shnuk* or *shnook* is a timid, meek, ineffectual, unassertive individual. Shnooks are, Rosten says, pathetic but likable; if they weren't likable, they would be described as *shmucks*. A *shloomp* is a drip, a drag, a wet blanket, and very close to being a creep. *Paskudnyaks* are mean, nasty, petty, and vulgar individuals.

The Old World Jews made the same types of distinctions between varieties of fools that American high school students do when they describe the kinds of students one finds in a typical high school: nerds, dorks, dweebs, preppies, white punks on dope, surfers, skaters, punks, and so on.

Schlimazels are often seen as very close to schlemiels. Everything a schlimazel does ends up disastrously—because the schlimazel has bad luck, not because he lacks intelligence or enterprise. As a twelfth-century schlimazel, a poet named Abraham ibn Ezra, put it:

If I sold shrouds,
No one would die.
If I sold lamps,
Then in the sky
The sun, for spite,
Would shine by night.

This notion that the fates are stacked against one is echoed in the following joke.

The Threat
A schlimazel demanded money from a wealthy man.
"You must give me money," insisted the schlimazel.
"Why must I?" asked the man.
"If you don't," said the schlimazel, "I'll go into the hat business!"
"So what?"
"So what? If a man with my luck goes into the hat business, all the babies in the country will be born without heads."

We find the same theme in the following schlimazel joke:

The Rabbi's Advice
A schlimazel was ushered in to see a rabbi famed for his wisdom and his practical advice.

> "You've got to help me, rabbi," said the schlimazel. "Whatever I try, fails. If I start selling umbrellas, it stops raining. If I sell shrouds, nobody dies. What should I do?"
>
> "Take my advice," says the rabbi, "and become a baker. If you become a baker you'll always, at the very least, have bread to put on the table."
>
> "That's true," said the schlimazel, "but what if I don't even have enough money to buy flour?"
>
> "Then you won't be a baker," replied the rabbi.

The rabbi's realism, "then you won't be a baker," is typical of many of the conclusions of many jokes. Many Jewish jokes end with understatements as "punch lines." The humor isn't a shock with some remarkable new line of direction but a kind of letdown, an ironic resolution.

In the following joke we see the same thing.

Life Is Like a Glass of Tea

> Goldberg and Cohen were in a café, drinking tea. After a pause, Goldberg said to Cohen, "You know . . . life is like a glass of tea."
>
> "Life is like a glass of tea? How do you explain this?" asked Cohen.
>
> "How should I know?" said Goldberg. "I'm not a philosopher."

When Goldberg is asked to explain his seemingly profound statement, "Life is like a glass of tea," he can't; it was just something that he said because it sounded profound. This is very similar to a joke about a rabbi who says, "Life is like a bathtub." When challenged to support this notion, the rabbi then says, "Okay, life isn't like a bathtub." These jokes poke fun at sages who supposedly offer wisdom but really are frauds.

THE SHADKEN

A *shadken* is a marriage broker, and it is the Herculean task of *shadkens*, in the classic Jewish jokes about them, to marry off women who are deaf, blind, lame, hunchbacked, and grossly deformed. Let me offer some *shadken* jokes here, before I discuss the significance of the *shadken* figure.

A Woman with One Fault
The shadken *was defending the girl he had proposed against the young man's protests. "I don't care for her mother-in-law," said the latter. "She's a disagreeable, stupid person." "But after all, you're not marrying the mother-in-law. What you want is her daughter." "Yes," said the young man, "but she's not young any longer, and she's not precisely a beauty." "No matter," said the* shadken. *"If she's neither young nor beautiful, she'll be more faithful to you." "And she hasn't much money." "Who's talking about money?" said the* shadken. *"Are you marrying a woman for money? What you want is a wife." "But she's got a hunchback, too." "Well, what do you want?" replied the* shadken. *"Isn't she to have a single fault?"*

The ironic nature of this punch line, which asks, after an endless list of the "deficiencies" of this woman, "Isn't she to have a single fault?" is very funny. Freud uses this joke in his book and points out that at each point the *shadken* makes the best of the problem. If the woman is ugly, the man won't have to worry about her being unfaithful, and so on. This is, Freud suggests, "pseudo-logic," in which the *shadken* isolated each defect and then pretended they all didn't exist when he argued, at the end, that the woman had only one fault—her hunchback.

Here's another *shadken* joke with the same kind of reasoning done by the *shadken*:

A Minor Fault
A shadken *told a young man, who was a potential client, about a girl he could offer him, a young woman named Shoshana. "Shoshana?" said the man. "That's ridiculous. She's almost blind." "That's a blessing," said the* shadken. *"She won't see, most of the time, what you're doing." "But she also stutters." "That's good luck for you," said the* shadken. *"If she stutters she won't talk too much, and will let you live in peace." "She's also deaf," replied the man. "I should have such luck," said the* shadken. *"If she's deaf, you can shout at her, you can bawl her out and not have to worry about her talking back." "But she's more than twenty years older than I am," said the young man. "I thought you were a man of vision," said the* shadken. *"I offer you this wonderful woman and you pick on one minor fault."*

Let me offer one more, which is a composite of several *shadken* jokes.

You Don't Have to Whisper
A shadken *brings a young man to the market to see a woman to consider for marriage. As they draw near, the* shadken *points out the woman. "But she's*

bleary-eyed and can hardly see." "So she won't notice your faults." "And she has a limp." "Only when she walks," replies the shadken. *As they draw near, the man whispers to the* shadken, *"And she's a hunchback, too." "You don't have to whisper," says the* shadken. *"She's deaf, too."*

In this joke, we have the *shadken* minimizing the faults of the poor woman he is trying to marry off, but he also points out yet another problem with the woman, offering what might be described as a "topper."

Let me suggest a few things about these *shadken* jokes. First, if we look at these jokes metaphorically, the grotesque women can be seen to represent the problems that Jews face in hostile environments. These women have everything against them, just like the *shadkens*, who must try to marry them off, and just like the Jews, who find themselves hated and relatively powerless.

On the more personal level, these jokes contain an expectancy on the part of the poor bleary-eyed, deaf, hunchbacked women that they can find a partner and be married, just like everyone else. There is a kind of optimism on the part of the women that, against great odds, they can succeed, somehow—with a little help from *shadkens*. They may be physically deformed and handicapped, but in a society of fools, anything is possible.

These jokes ridicule the search for perfection, for an "ideal wife," by focusing on the opposite—imperfect women who have a variety of afflictions. The women the *shadken* has to marry off are, almost without exception, ugly, old, deaf, blind, hunchbacked, and they walk with a limp.

But the *shadken* "rationalizes" all these defects and either turns them into assets or minimizes them. In one *shadken* joke, the woman the *shadken* is trying to marry off actually is beautiful, but, as it turns out, "slightly pregnant." So she, too, is damaged goods. Nevertheless, despite incredible odds, the *shadken* persists—always optimistic, always hopeful, generally explaining away this or that deformity in his customers.

One other thing we notice in these *shadken* jokes: they tend to show *shadkens* trying to sell men on the "virtues" of women who are invariably ugly, blind, hunchbacked, and so on. There is, I would suggest, a subconscious hostility toward women reflected in these jokes. If the women aren't deformed, they are "slightly pregnant," or something else is wrong with them. I can't recall any jokes about beautiful women being taken by *shadkens* to meet ugly and deformed men. On the other hand, the extreme degree to which these women are impaired makes the jokes almost surrealistic and gives them a sense of unreality.

We see, then, in most of these jokes, a tendency in *shadkens* (who I suggest can be seen as symbolic figures representing Jews in general) a tendency to make the best they can of the calamities they face. Perhaps, in some cases, *shadkens* (as symbolic Jews) lack the ability to see the problems they face or to recognize the dimensions of their problems. This inability to see reality at its darkest, or perhaps ugliest is a better term, may explain the optimism found in Jews—and *shadkens*.

THE SCHNORRER

Schnorrers, according to Ausubel, were somewhat different from traditional beggars. As he explains (1978, 267):

> ... It might be well to point out that the psychological makeup of the *schnorrer*, or for that matter of any other Jewish type, was not due to anything innately peculiar to the character of the Jewish people, but was due rather to the peculiar conditions with which Jewish life was burdened for so many centuries.
>
> What were the characteristics of the *schnorrer*? He disdained to stretch out his hand for alms like an ordinary beggar. He did not solicit aid—he demanded it. . . . Since he was obliged to live by his wits he, understandably enough, developed all the facile improvisations of an adventurer. To reach his objective, he considered all means fair. Tact and self-restraint were not his strong points; they would only prove practical stumbling blocks to the practice of his "profession." Next to his adroitness in fleecing the philanthropic sheep was his *chutzpah*, his unmitigated arrogance.

Ausubel makes several important points here. First, he argues that the schnorrer and other comic Jewish types are not due to psychological peculiarities of individuals but were a response to the extremely difficult situations in which people in the shtetls and other Jewish communities found themselves.

Schnorrering should be seen, then, as an adaptation for survival and is, then, the consequence of social and political conditions. The schnorrer is a professional fleecer of philanthropists and relies on certain characteristics to function effectively: cleverness and chutzpah. Ausubel defines chutzpah as arrogance, but there are other aspects to the term. Rosten adds terms like gall, effrontery, presumption-plus-arrogance, and incredible "guts." There is something almost heroic about the audacity of the schnorrer.

One thing we should recognize is that schnorrers played an important part in the life of the shtetl, and many schnorrers had regular routes which, people said jokingly, they passed on at death to their successors or gave as gifts for their daughters' dowry. Mark Zborowski and Elizabeth Herzog discuss the role of the schnorrer in *Life Is with People* (1952, 211):

> The beggar is an important member of the shtetl. He is everywhere, in the market, in the shul, invited to weddings where special tables are set for him. . . . The respectable inhabitant of the shtetl may despise the schnorrers, but he is cowed by their rages and their expletives. The schnorrer is an artist in curses, producing the most elaborate and sophisticated examples on the slightest provocation, especially if one refuses or gives less than expected.
>
> It is not only the verbal violence that intimidates the schnorrer's benefactors, however. He presents the extreme example of an interdependence evident in any recipient-donor relationship of the shtetl. Despised and faceless, the beggar nevertheless feels himself at an advantage, because the more fortunate need him as an object of charity. It is he who opens for them the portals of heaven.

Schnorrers (or *shnorrers*, to use another spelling of the term) are integrated into the community and play a role. Judaism's ethic of looking after the poor and hungry give the schnorrer a place in the scheme of things.

Here are some schnorrer jokes that show the impudence and other personality characteristics of typical schnorrers.

Bread and Challah

A woman invited a schnorrer into her kitchen to feed him. On the table were plates with black bread and with challah. The schnorrer started eating the challah, and paid no attention to the black bread. So the woman said, "there's black bread, too." "I like the challah better," said the schnorrer. "But the challah is very expensive," said the woman. "And well worth it," replied the schnorrer.

The ironic sense that only the best is good enough for those who have nothing is a common thread in schnorrer jokes.

The Clinic

A schnorrer appeared at the home of a rich man and begged for some money to see a doctor. The rich man gave him some money. "But I need more than this if I'm to go to the clinic." "But that's very expensive," said the rich man. "Why don't you go to a regular doctor?" "For my health," said the schnorrer, "nothing is too good."

In the joke that follows, we also see the notion that schnorrers provide for others.

The Inheritance

A schnorrer had appeared at a rich man's house every Friday for years for the Sabbath meal. One Friday a young man appeared with the schnorrer. The host was put out by this. "Who's this?" he asked. "I should have told you," said the schnorrer. "It's my new son-in-law. I promised him board for the first year of his marriage."

Schnorrers are impudent and full of chutzpah because they recognize that they play an important role in the scheme of things: making it possible for Jews to discharge their religious obligations toward those less fortunate than themselves. There is something almost heroic in their chutzpah and sense of professionalism, given the reality of their destitution. They were, like so many of the comic types found in Jewish jokes and folklore, people who lived by their wits or, in other cases, lack of wits.

AN ASIDE ON AMERICAN JEWISH HUMOR AND KINDS OF CONGREGATIONS

There is an amusing article, "Denominationitis," that appeared in the bulletin of Young Israel of Hollywood-Fort Lauderdale, Florida (and was reprinted in the February 1983 edition of *Young Israel Viewpoints*) and makes fun of the differences between various American Jewish denominations in South Florida—and in America, by extension. This humor uses the techniques of description and exaggeration to satirize the numerous kinds of temples that one finds in some Jewish communities.

1. *Ultra-Orthodox.* Yarmulkas worn; all male members expected to know Hebrew and Yiddish; separate seating with the balcony of 6-foot mechitza; all members observe Shabbat and Kashrut; State of Israel frowned upon.
2. *Traditional Orthodox.* Yarmulkas; congregants wear modern clothing; recognize State of Israel; mechitza; no

mixed dancing permitted; talking during davening mandatory (except for the rabbi).
3. *Modern Orthodox.* Yarmulkas; men and women sit apart but women are respected; only older men know Hebrew; congregants observe Kashrut at home; rabbi shaves; mixed dancing when rabbi is not looking.
4. *Traditional Conservative.* No mechitza; yarmulkas; use a different prayer book; "kashrut" observed in synagogue only; congregants must either give money, attend services, or at least go once to Israel on the rabbi's tour.
5. *Centrist Conservative.* Rabbi and cantor expected to know Hebrew; rabbi drives to services.
6. *Liberal Conservative.* Yarmulkas worn if desired; cash donations accepted on the Sabbath; Kashrut discussed in adult education classes; choir may include non-Jews.
7. *Traditional Reform.* Same as above; rabbi must be Jewish; choir may include blacks; janitor must wear Yarmulka.
8. *Reconstructionist.* Yarmulkas worn at services; rabbi is secularist; details of the ritual practice optional and dependent on rabbi's mood and current events.
9. *Moderate Reform.* Rabbi must have Ph.D. in some branch of humanities and play tennis; no Yarmulkas; Sabbath candles lit in temple; rabbi willing to share pulpit with liberal Protestant minister; will perform intermarriage if couple signs paper promising to raise children Jewish.
10. *Liberal Reform.* Very similar to Unitarian Church; rabbi need not be Jewish, but must like Jewish food.

This little bit of humor is not too far removed from the joke about the Jews arguing whose temple was the most progressive. You end up with one kind of congregation of Jewnitarians in which the rabbi doesn't even have to be Jewish—but he (or she) *must* like Jewish food. Even though Judaism tends to have three major divisions: Orthodox, Conservative, and Reform congregations, there are various modifications of each of these branches, and other kinds of congregations as well.

We can see that in the New World (as well as the Old), Judaism, its institutions, and various kinds of Jews still remain a core subject of Jewish humor. And hovering in the background in this list of congregations is the problem Jews always face—assimilation and loss of identity.

5

Jokes about Jews and Ethnic and Racial Minorities

Jews aren't the only people who make jokes about Jews. There are numerous jokes (and by jokes I'm including riddles, even though technically they aren't jokes) non-Jews make about Jews and other ethnic minorities as well, just as Jews make jokes about members of other ethnic minorities or retell jokes that others have made. Freud took notice of this phenomenon and commented about it in his *Jokes and Their Relation to the Unconscious*. He wrote (Norton, 1963, originally published in German in 1905):

> A particularly favourable occasion for tendentious jokes is presented when the intended rebellious criticism is directed against the subject himself, or, to put it more cautiously, against someone in whom the subject has a share—a collective person, that is (the subject's own nation, for instance). The occurrence of self-criticism as a determinant may explain how it is that a number of

the most apt jokes (of which we have given plenty of instances) have grown up on the soil of Jewish popular life. They are stories created by Jews and directed against Jewish characteristics. The jokes made about Jews by foreigners are for the most part brutal comic stories in which a joke is made unnecessary by the fact that Jews are regarded by foreigners as comic figures.

Freud distinguishes, then, between jokes Jews tell about themselves and jokes others tell about Jews, the latter often being "brutal comic stories."

Recent research by Richard Raskin confirms Freud's insights. As he explained, after a five-year study of Jewish jokes, "Jokes told by Jews about Jews are affectionate, but those told from outside the community often carry sinister anti-Semitic overtones" (Dateline *World Jewry*, Feb. 1990). These jokes, which are often hostile and anti-Semitic, can be thought of as reflecting "ascribed deflation" of the Jews, in contrast, for example, to ascribed status.

JOKES ABOUT JEWS BY NON-JEWS

Another researcher, folklorist Alan Dundes, offers a number of jokes told by non-Jews about Jews (in an article entitled "A Study of Ethnic Slurs: The Jew and the Polack in the United States," reprinted in his book *Cracking Jokes*). He lists a number of the stereotypes of Jews that are found in these jokes. He also points out that members of ethnic groups often enjoy telling negative and hostile jokes about their own ethnic group.

I will list a number of the stereotypes which, Dundes suggests, are generally picked up through folklore, and offer some examples of humor (since they aren't always jokes, technically speaking) for each category. In some cases, we have jokes that Jews make up about themselves, but in others we have rather insulting and nasty jokes told by non-Jews about Jews.

A Concern with Making Money

Jesus saves, Moses invests.

Have you heard the Jewish football yell? It goes "get that quarter back."

How do they take a census in Israel? They roll a nickel down the street.

When Billy Graham sang "All I Want Is Jesus," ten thousand people joined the Protestant church. When Pope Pius sang "Ave Maria," twenty thousand people joined the Catholic church. When Pat Boone sang "There's a Gold Mine in the Sky," a hundred thousand Jews joined the air force.

In these jokes, Jews are basically motivated by making money, unlike other people, that is Christians, who are motivated by higher principles—love of Jesus or Mary.

Always Looking for a Bargain or Trying to Make a Sale

This is station KVY, Tel Aviv, 1800 on your dial—but for you, 1795.

The KYV joke alludes to the penchant Jews have for buying things wholesale or at bargain prices.

A Protestant, a Negro, and a Jew die and go to Heaven. When they get there, St. Peter says to the Protestant, "What do you want?" The Protestant says "Nice food, a nice pasture, and some nice sheep." St. Peter then asks the Negro what he wants. The Negro says "A big, flashy Cadillac, a million dollars, and a big white house." St. Peter then asks the Jew what he wants, and the Jew replies, "All you've got to give me is a suitcase full of trinkets and the address of that Negro!"

It is suggested in this joke that Negroes (or African-Americans in more modern terms) are materialistic and relatively stupid and that they are taken advantage of by Jews. The Jew could have asked for anything he wanted, but he chose, instead, to fleece the Negro of what he had. This joke reflects an attitude found in some African-Americans that their worst enemies are the Jews, who are also blamed for slavery and a host of other ills.

A Desire for Status, Often Achieved by Men Becoming Professional Men and by Women Marrying Professional Men

What did Mr. Mink give Mrs. Mink for Christmas? A full-length Jew.

This joke deals with the trait in some middle-class Jews of buying mink coats for their wives as a sign of their wealth and success. It is based on the technique of reversal: instead of the Jew buying the full-length mink coat, the mink buys a full-length Jew.

> *What's the definition of a CPA (Certified Public Accountant)? It's a Jewish boy who can't stand the sight of blood and who stutters.*

This riddle alludes to another well-known companion riddle that is based on the propensity of many Jewish males to enter the professions. One reason for this, I should point out, is that due to anti-Semitism, it was not possible for Jews to enter, let alone succeed, in many businesses and other kinds of organizations (or, in earlier years in Eastern Europe, to farm, go into business, and so on).

For example, many English departments in American universities, until thirty or forty years ago, kept Jews out. Another reason for the large number of Jews in the professions is that Jews have traditionally stressed the importance of education. And having a profession gives one mobility in case it is necessary to leave an area, something that I would suggest exists subliminally in the consciousness of Jews, even in democratic societies like the United States.

> *What do you call a Jewish boy who can't stand the sight of blood? A lawyer.*

When you add stuttering to not being able to stand the sight of blood, which means the boy cannot become a doctor or a lawyer, you get the CPA.

Doctors seems to have the highest status in the Jewish pantheon of professions, as the following joke suggests.

My Son, the President
A Jewish man is elected president of the United States. After six months in office, he calls his mother, who lives in Miami. "Mother," he says, "I'd like to have you come and visit me in the White House." "Vy not?" says his mother. The president arranges for Air Force One to fly to Miami and pick up his mother. When she lands, a long limousine is at the airport to take her to the White House. When the limousine pulls into the gate at the White House, the guard says to her, "You must know someone important to get this treatment." "Yes," she says. "The President is the brother of my son, the doctor!"

In this joke, it is the fact that one of her sons is a doctor that is the important thing to this woman, not the fact that her other son is President of the United States. Medicine, it should be pointed out, was, for many centuries, one of the few professions Jews were allowed to practice, and it is reasonable to suggest that the high status doctors had and have are a significant element in these doctor jokes.

Jews Have Big Noses

On the Origin of Jewish Noses
Why do Jews have big noses?
Air is free.

This joke also deals with another stereotype, discussed earlier—that Jews are cheap and always looking for bargains.

> **The Monster**
> What happened when the Jewish woman took Thalidomide?
> She gave birth to a ten-pound nose.

We have here a somewhat surrealistic joke, like the one about the mink giving his wife a full-length Jew. Jews are turned into big noses as the result of a woman taking Thalidomide when pregnant. This is related to disaster jokes, an important genre of jokes that seem to spontaneously arise after major disasters such as the *Challenger* explosion that killed seven astronauts.

Propensity for Pro-Semitism

> **Babe Ruth's Sixtieth Home Run**
> One day, when Babe Ruth was the hero of every boy in America, little Bennie came running in to his grandfather and yelled, excitedly, "Grandfather, grandfather ... Babe Ruth just hit his sixtieth home run this season." His grandfather looked at him and asked, "So—how is this going to help the Jews?"

I've also heard this joke with the punch line, "So—is this good for the Jews?" The point, here, is that according to the stereotype, Jews are so concerned about Judaism and "The Jewish Question" that they look at everything in terms of how it relates to the Jews. This characteristic, I would suggest, is not unique to the Jews; it tends to be seen in small ethnic minorities that are anxiety-ridden about maintaining their ethnic identities and cultural traditions.

A Tendency to Conceal One's Jewishness and to Assimilate

> ### The New Catholic
> *A little old devout Orthodox Jew decided in the latter part of his life to convert to Catholicism. The Catholic Church was delighted, because they saw this as wonderful propaganda for the universal appeal of the Church, and so a priest invited him to speak at the next service. So the little Jew got up and said, "Fellow goyim . . . "*

This joke is really about assimilation but involves concealment of Jewishness as well. Assimilation and concealment are done by casting off one's Jewish identity or joining a different religious organization, or, in some cases, both. Jews want to conceal their Jewish identity, so their jokes suggest, for a variety of reasons: because they are ashamed of being Jewish or tired of being in a small minority. In some jokes, the Jew who wants to convert has yet a different reason.

> ### The Convert
> *An old Jewish man is dying. He says to his son, "Go, call a Catholic priest. I want to convert!" "What?" says the son. "Have you gone out of your mind?" "Listen," says the father, "better one of them than one of us."*

In this joke, the father—using the twisted logic we find in many Jewish jokes—thinks it is better for a Catholic to die than a Jew, and so decides to convert.

Let me offer another well-known joke on this subject.

The Hotel in Florida
A wealthy Jew and his wife take a plane to Florida, hop a cab to a very fancy hotel, and go inside to register. There is a sign saying "No Jews Allowed" on the wall above the registration desk. The clerk looks at them suspiciously. "Your name?" he asks. "Mr. and Mrs. Ross," they answer. He listens to their accent. "You're not Jewish, by any chance, are you?" he inquires. The Rosses don't want to bother going to another hotel, so they tell him they aren't Jewish. "We're Methodists," they say. "Okay," says the clerk. "You can have room 120. That will be two hundred and fifty dollars a night." At this, the woman says "Oy . . . whatever that means."

Here the ability of the Jews to disguise their Jewishness is not very effective.

Dundes, who happens to be Jewish, summarizes his findings about the way Jews are stereotyped in the following manner:

> There is an endless amount of Jewish humor and the present sampling is merely to delineate various features of the stereotype of the Jew in American folklore. The principal traits are obvious enough: the concern with money, trade, status, professionalism, the large nose, the undesirability and, in fact, impossibility of renouncing one's ethnic identity as a Jew, a prideful consciousness of the Judaic elements in Christianity, and a fear for the loss of ethnic identity through marriage with gentiles.

Some of the traits that are associated with Jews, Dundes points out, are associated with other ethnic groups, but you don't find the whole collection of traits.

Scots, for example, may be stereotyped as thrifty, cheap, and canny, but they aren't portrayed as having big noses or being overly concerned with professionalism or the "Scottish question." Let me offer some typical Scottish jokes:

The Accident in Edinburgh
Did you hear about the accident in Edinburgh last week?
Two cabs collided and twenty Scots were injured.

This riddle alludes to their cheapness; there were, it turns out, ten Scots in each cab.

Interestingly enough, I find that many of my students are not aware of this stereotype of Scots and thus don't "get" the riddle until I explain things. The next joke adds craftiness to cheapness:

The Escape
Three Scots were in church when the minister announced he was sending around a plate for the collection. At this, one Scot yelled "Aaaah" and pretended to faint. The other two Scots carried him out of the church, saying, "He needs some fresh air."

The cheapness of the Scots, unlike the cheapness of the Jews, is not considered a serious flaw in their character, and their craftiness is admired, whereas the shrewdness and craftiness of the Jews is seen negatively.

ITALIAN JOKES THAT ITALIAN-AMERICANS TELL ABOUT THEMSELVES

A number of years ago, a baby-sitter of mine, who happened to be a young Italian-American woman, told me a number of jokes (actually riddles, which is the form much ethnic humor takes) that she said Italian-Americans told about themselves. We must remember that when an ethnic tells a joke about his or her ethnic group, it is quite different than when someone from a different ethnic or other group tells the joke. People from within an ethnic group are entitled, we tend to feel, to make fun of themselves, and this is seen as relatively harmless.

ITALIAN-AMERICAN JOKES

What is red, yellow, orange, green, blue, and purple?
An Italian dressed up.

Why don't Italians kill flies?
Flies are the Italian national bird.

Who wears a long, dirty white flowing robe and rides a pig?
Lawrence of Italy.

How can you tell the bride at an Italian wedding?
The hair under her armpits is braided.

Why do Italians wear pointed shoes?
To kill cockroaches when they retreat into corners.

Who won the Italian beauty contest?
Nobody.

What happened when Israel declared war on Egypt?
Italy surrendered.

Who shot the five bullets that killed Mussolini?
Five hundred Italian marksmen.

Who is in the smallest book in the library?
Italian war heroes.

Why do Italian tanks have three reverse speeds and one forward speed?
The forward speed is in case the tanks are attacked from the rear.

These stereotypes are typical of the way Italians used to be seen by many people a number of generations ago, when Americans (all immigrants themselves, mind you) looked down upon Italians and thought of them as essentially peasants. Italians also are stereotyped as not being valiant fighters—or to put it more directly, cowards. There's a wonderful riddle on this subject:

What's the difference between Israelis and Italians?
Israelis are wonderful fighters and terrible waiters.

You are left to supply the rest of the answer.

These jokes represent, I would suggest, a sense of inferiority and a sense of anxiety about having an Italian-American identity in second-generation Italian-Americans, and thus indicate a desire to integrate (and assimilate) into

American culture at large. That is, the jokes reflect a desire to drop the Italian part of Italian-American, to the extent that this is possible. This was, after all, one of the basic functions of the American education system—to turn immigrants into "real" Americans. In contemporary American society, in which ethnicity is now seen positively, the situation would be different, though jokes about Italians as cowards are still common.

ELEPHANT JOKES AS DISGUISED ANTI-NEGRO JOKES

Alan Dundes and Roger Abrahams have suggested, in a controversial article, "On Elephantasy and Elephanticide: The Effect of Time and Place," that elephant riddles are really, among other things, disguised attacks on African-Americans. Their article combines psychoanalytic interpretation with sociopolitical analysis. I will offer a sampling of these riddles from a large number of elephant riddles they use in their article:

ELEPHANT JOKES

How do you know when an elephant's in bed with you?
Nine months later you have a problem.

How do elephants make love in the water?
They take their trunks down.

What's the difference between a saloon and an elephant fart?
One's a bar-room; the other is more of a BarOOOMM!

*How do you keep an elephant
   from charging?
You take away his credit card.*

*What is harder than getting a
   pregnant elephant in a Volkswagen?
Getting an elephant pregnant in a Volkswagen.*

*What did the elephant say after the alligator bit off
   his trunk?
(Nasally) Very funny!*

The authors point out that there is a considerable amount of sexual content to these jokes involving Oedipal conflicts, which must be kept in mind. (The alligator joke, for example, involves symbolic castration, and many of the jokes involve controlling this powerful animal, one way or another.)

They also argue that there is a reason this cycle of jokes arose when it did, and to understand such cycles, we must keep in mind the "social-historical context" in which we find these jokes. Elephant jokes became popular at the same time the black freedom movement was developing, and these jokes, the authors suggest, involve disguised ways of dealing with anxieties caused by this movement.

As they write (Dundes, 1987, 54):

> The development of the black freedom movement, causing anxiety even among those sympathetic to the movement, would seem to be the catalytic agent producing such a regressive response. There is no inconsistency in arguing that the elephant may be both the adult sexual

rival of the child and the black sexual rival of the white. Both rivals represent power, in part sexual, which threatens and which must therefore be conquered. It is easier to conquer in fantasy than in reality. If killing the elephant eliminates either the father, the black, or both, and if it accomplishes it harmlessly under cover of nonsense so that the killer need feel no guilt, then the function and significance of elephant jokes are clear. These jokes, like all expressions of wit, are serious business.

Thus elephant jokes are more significant than we might imagine, since they enable those who tell the jokes to take care of pressing psychological needs under cover of nonsense, and thus escape the strictures of the superego. We see, then, that in some cases humor enables people to disguise their aggressive feelings and deal with anxieties of which they are unaware. Let me conclude this segment with an elephant joke that was not in the Dundes and Abrahams article:

What the Elephant Said to the Naked Man
What did the elephant say to the naked man?
How do you get enough to eat with that*?*

Here we see that there is a sexual content to this joke, as the elephant compares his trunk with the man's penis, mistakenly thinking that it is used to secure food (though in some cases, ironically, it is—but not in the same manner).

POLISH STEREOTYPES

There were a number of Polish jokes and riddles that became very popular for a while. Many of these Polish jokes and riddles, I should point out, are told by the British about the Irish.

POLISH JOKES

What is Polish matched luggage like?
Shopping bags from the same supermarket.

Why is the Polish suicide rate so low?
It's hard to commit suicide jumping out of a basement window.

What has an IQ of 450?
Poland.

How many Poles does it take to change a light bulb?
Five. One to hold the bulb and four to turn the table on which he's standing.

Who won the Polish beauty contest?
Nobody. (This joke, we see, is also used in ethnic humor about Italians.)

Why does the Pope have TGIF painted on his slippers?
To remind him, "Toes Go In First."

Let me offer a wonderful joke, not a riddle, about the alleged stupidity of Poles.

Shopping for Brains
A man went out shopping in the market for brains he wanted to serve at dinner that night. In the butcher shop, there were all kinds of brains from different

ethnic groups: French brains, $1.00 a pound; English brains $1.20 a pound; German brains $1.25 a pound; Greek brains, $1.35 a pound; and Polish brains, $5.75 a pound. "Why are the Polish brains so much more expensive than all of the other brains?" he asked. "Because," said the butcher, "Sometimes we have to go through ten or even twelve Poles before we find a brain!"

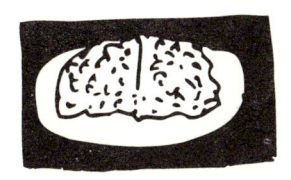

The Polish joke about light bulbs probably led to the light bulb riddle, which functioned as an all-purpose means of attacking various groups and ethnic minorities.

LIGHT BULB JOKES

In these jokes, various ethnic, social, political, religious, and other groups are ridiculed about the way they screw in light bulbs. Here are some examples.

How many Jews does it take to screw in a light bulb?
So, how many Jews does it take?

This joke makes fun of the Jewish propensity to answer a question with another question.

How many JAPs does it take to screw in a light bulb?
Two. One to get the diet Pepsis and the other to call Daddy.

How many Jewish mothers does it take to screw in a light bulb?
"Don't bother. I'll sit here in the dark!"

Here the Jewish mother's desire not to trouble anyone, especially her sons, and to suffer willingly, is ridiculed.

How many psychiatrists does it take to screw in a light bulb?
One. But the light bulb has to sincerely want to change.

How many Marxists does it take to screw in a proletarian light bulb?
None. Proletarian light bulbs contain the seeds of their own revolutions.

How many Blacks does it take to screw in a light bulb?
Hey, motherfucker . . . whatsa light bulb?

How many residents of Marin County (famed as an "I want it now" bastion of hedonism) does it take to screw in a light bulb?

People from Marin County don't screw in light bulbs, they screw in hot tubs.

Dundes, in an article titled "Many Hands Make Light Work, or Caught in the Act of Screwing in Light Bulbs," suggests that these jokes have to do with unconscious feelings of powerlessness and also reflect the "age-old theme of sexual impotence," which are reflected in all the different groups seeking power and the malaise Americans felt about the energy crisis at the end of the 1970s (1987, 148,149). The term *screwing* has obvious sexual connotations that tend to be hidden by the silliness of the different ways people screw in light bulbs or the problems they face in doing or not doing so.

These riddles are very similar in nature to what might be described as "national character jokes," jokes about the way different nationalities do things, which use the techniques of stereotyping and theme and variation. Thus there are many jokes about what members of different nationalities say after they've had sex:

Jewish Girl: *Next time I'll hold out for a mink coat!*
American Girl: *I must have been drunk. What did you say your name was?*
French Girl: *I'll get a new dress, for this, oui?*
English Girl: *This was most pleasant. We must meet again.*
Russian Girl: *You've had my body, but my soul will always be mine.*

Another set of jokes deals with the difference between paradise and hell, playing with stereotypes of various nationalities.

Paradise and Hell

Paradise is where the cooks are French, the waiters are Italian, the mechanics are German, and the police are English. Hell is where the police are German, the cooks are English, the waiters are French, and the mechanics are Italian.

These jokes deal with commonly held notions about the temperaments and talents of different nationalities. Most ethnic humor, however, deals with the stupidity of various groups. Americans tell jokes about Poles being stupid and people from England tell the same jokes (in many cases) about people from Ireland being stupid.

Jokes about ethnic groups being stupid are, as Christie Davies points out, very common. As he explains in *Ethnic Humor Around the World* (1990, 10):

> Although the ethnic jokes told in many societies through the world pin a wide range of comic attributes onto a great variety of peoples and ethnic groups, one pair of ethnic jokes seems to be far more widespread, more numerous, and more durable than any other. This pair comprises on the one hand jokes about groups depicted as stupid, inept, and ignorant . . . and on the other, as if in opposition, jokes about groups portrayed as canny, calculating, and craftily stingy. Such jokes far outnumber jokes based on any other comic trait ascribed to any group of people, whether nation, ethnic group, or regional minority.

These jokes are found everywhere, and have, among other functions, many of which have been discussed in other chapters, giving tellers a vicarious sense of superiority over the group being ridiculed for its stupidity. Of course, being more intelligent than stupid people doesn't mean that much, but we take our pleasures and satisfactions where we can get them. Davies suggests that stupidity becomes significant now because we live in modern, technologically advanced, information societies, where a premium is placed on one's intelligence, rationality, and similar matters. Stupidity is a matter that poses problems for those who are dominant and are in the "center" of things and "is a quality best comically banished to the periphery and located safely in some other group" (1990, 20).

WHY THE RIDDLE?

Many of these "jokes," as I've mentioned a number of times, are not technically jokes—short humorous stories with punch lines—but riddles. Riddles are comic questions that are posed to people and zany or absurd answers to the questions. There is a "contest" element to the riddle: you are asked a question to see whether you know the answer. If you do, you "win," so to speak—which means the comic element is no longer operative.

In a sense, the answer to the riddle is like a punch line in a joke. It is the answer to the riddle that generates the laughter or humor. The question becomes a foreshortened version of what could be a joke, except that instead of many joke elements, there is only one. Ethnic riddles also generate a play frame that suggests that what is being related is humorous and not serious, so the insults are, in theory, "not to be taken seriously." In reality, ethnic minorities who are the victims of jokes and riddles often become extremely insulted and, as ethnic minorities have gained power, the use of riddles and other ethnic humor in public performances (or by public figures such as politicians) has become unacceptable.

Riddles rely on the general absurdity of their answers and techniques such as exaggeration, facetiousness, and insult, along with stereotyping, to create their effects. As I pointed out earlier, to work, riddles rely on the ignorance of the person being asked the question, so there is something ironic about people who are "made ignorant" by the riddle laughing at Poles and others for being stupid. It is the zany quality of the answers to riddles, which find endless new ways of insulting their victims, that is significant.

Riddles are also regressive and have been described by Dundes and Abrahams as (Dundes, 1987, 42): "a childish type of humor. It involves the simple, highly repetitive form of the conundrum, deriving a great deal of its humor from the restricted form and subject matter. Furthermore, the world presented in these jokes is whimsically topsy-turvy...." According to psychoanalytic theory, we often enjoy regressions as a temporary relief from the burdens of adulthood, from societal restraints and the burdens of the superego; thus regression is a useful and a perfectly normal phenomenon. Dundes and Abrahams quote Freud on this matter (1987, 42): "Under the influence of the comic, we return to the happiness of childhood. We can throw off the fetters of logical thought and revel in long-forgotten freedom." This freedom generated by regression is, of course, just temporary. Regression also tends to be a response to anxiety, which is why Dundes and Abrahams suggest that anxieties about the black freedom movement could be manifested in the form of elephant jokes.

We can also look upon these ethnic riddles as parodies of the Socratic method. Socrates asked all kinds of questions, feigning ignorance, to help those he was dialoguing with discover knowledge and attain wisdom. Socrates was an *eiron* figure, a pretender who asked questions because he didn't seem to know the answers. In reality, these questions led people to see the errors in their thinking. Ethnic riddles, on the other hand, mock knowledge and wisdom and use the dialogue for nonsense expressions of hostility.

ON JEWISH JOKES AND JOKES ABOUT JEWS

Let me suggest we are dealing with two kinds of jokes here: there are *Jewish jokes*, told by Jews about Jews and others, and there are *jokes about Jews*, told by others, some of whom are anti-Semitic and others of whom enjoy the humor and perhaps don't recognize the degree of hostility in many of these jokes. What are the functions of these jokes about Jews? Let me offer some suggestions, recognizing that my points don't apply to all jokes about Jews.

Jokes about Jews tend to focus upon negative stereotypes of Jews and don't reflect positively on Jews, Judaism, the attainments of Jews, or positive aspects about Jews: their ethical qualities, their sense of obligation to others in their community (Jews are very generous in giving to charities, Jewish and non-Jewish), their achievements, and so on. These anti-Jewish jokes offer no insights into Jewish culture and character because they are not interested in such subjects; the focus is on attacking simplistic stereotypes, straw men and women, and using humor as a mask to justify the aggression.

Ironically, anti-Semitic jokes (and all forms of anti-Semitism) generate a stronger sense of identity in Jews. These jokes help "secure the boundaries," we might say, between Jews and others, between Judaism and Christianity, the dominant religion in the United States. Pressure from without helps those within unify and resist being attacked. It is the weakening of anti-Semitism in America and the rise of intermarriage and assimilation (the subject of many Jewish jokes) that are, arguably, the biggest problems American Jews face.

There is an element of projection in many of the jokes that suggest that Jews are inferior. Quite likely, it is a sense of inferiority on the part of those who tell anti-Semitic or anti-Jewish jokes that is the operative force behind them. That may be one reason why the notion that Jews are the "chosen" people is the subject of a number of anti-Jewish jokes and why many Jewish jokes involve Jewish accents. Jewish accents or dialects, from this perspective, are signifiers of one's inability or lack of desire to integrate into American culture and society. Mocking people for their accents gives the mocker, who can speak English without an accent (or without an accent that is looked down upon) a sense of superiority.

It may be, of course, that it is a good thing for people who are full of hostility and even hatred for Jews to tell anti-Semitic jokes rather than resort to violence. Verbal aggression can be seen as a functional alternative to physical violence, one that relieves individuals of severe aggressive tendencies. This is probably true, but there is also the matter of verbal hostility dehumanizing victims in the eyes of anti-Jewish joke tellers and possibly leading them to what they see as "justified" violence. Words hurt, but they don't hurt as much as sticks and stones, which break our bones, to recall and update the old song. So punch lines are to be preferred to punches.

There is a conflict, suggests one humor researcher, anthropologist Mahadeve L. Apte, between two American core values when it comes to ethnic humor. He defines ethnic humor as a kind of humor "in which fun is made of the perceived behavior, customs, personality, or any other traits of a group or its members by virtue of their specific socio-cultural identity" (Berger, 1987, 27). These two core values are having a good sense of humor, on the one hand, and being positive about ethnic and cultural pluralism, on the other hand.

The problem, as he points out, is that these two values conflict with each other when ethnic jokes are told, and as members of ethnic and other groups have developed an intolerance for being ridiculed, Americans have had to suppress—at least in the public domain—expressions of ethnic humor. It is impossible to stamp out ethnic humor in folklore, and people will always tell jokes and riddles about ethnic groups and other groups. In many cases, members of ethnic groups tell jokes about themselves. Thus Apte concludes:

> the initiation and use of ethnic humor, especially jokes, in contemporary American society has come under severe constraints. This state of affairs is the result of ambivalence created by the conflict between two core cultural values, namely having a sense of humor and emphasis on cultural pluralism. . . . The tendency to engage in ethnic humor, however, still persists in the private domain and in small-group interactions, as does the interest in reading ethnic humor and enjoying it in private.

There is a difference between Jewish ethnic humor and other forms of ethnic humor, suggests Martin Grotjahn, a psychiatrist who has written extensively on humor. As he suggests in his article, "Dynamics of Jewish Jokes" (Berger, 1987): "No other ethnic joke follows the dynamics of the Jewish joke. Other ethnic jokes are hidden insults against a racial or national group, and are without the triumphant turn of the Jewish joke."

It is to this subject—what is distinctive (if anything) about the Jewish joke and Jewish humor in general—and to theories about these matters, that we turn in the next chapter.

6

On the Question of Masochism and Other Aspects of Jewish Humor

Logically, a good argument could be made for my using this chapter to evaluate the various points made in the book. But there's also a good reason for using this chapter to end the book. Having exposed readers to a large number of Jewish jokes and to discussions and analyses of these jokes and other aspects of Jewish humor, a chapter on whether Jewish jokes are masochistic and other theoretical matters enables readers to evaluate better the theories various authors have offered about Jewish jokes and Jewish humor. I decided that it was advantageous to get right into the jokes and leave the theories for the end.

One of the biggest questions about Jewish humor involves the matter of whether this humor represents a masochistic aspect of the Jewish personality. I understand masochism to mean deriving pleasure from pain (often of a sexual nature) or, in social matters, being mistreated in some manner.

THE QUESTION OF MASOCHISM

In *Jokes and Their Relation to the Unconscious*, Freud makes a remark about Jewish humor that has led to a considerable amount of controversy. He wrote (1963, 113), "Incidentally, I do not know whether there are many other instances of a people making fun to such a degree of its own character." For some reason, this remark (and others as well) has led a number of writers and scholars to suggest that Jewish humor is masochistic and not a healthy phenomenon.

Let me offer a joke by Freud that will have some significance here. He is talking about what he describes as a subspecies of indirect representation—how something trivial or small can be used to represent something large by means of a minor detail. He offers the following story (which could easily be seen as a joke) (1963, 80):

The Jew on the Train
A Galician Jew was traveling in a train. He had made himself really comfortable, had unbuttoned his coat and put his feet up on the seat. Just then a gentleman in modern dress entered the compartment. The Jew promptly pulled himself together and took up a proper pose. The stranger fingered through the pages of a notebook, made some calculations, reflected for a moment, and then suddenly asked the Jew, "Excuse me, when is Yom Kippur (the Day

of Atonement)?" "Oho!" said the Jew, and put his feet upon on the seat again before answering.

Freud follows his remark about Jews making fun of themselves as follows (1963, 113):

> As an example of this I may take the anecdote, quoted on p. 80 f., of a Jew on a railway train promptly abandoning all decent behavior when he discovered that the newcomer into his apartment was a fellow-believer. We made the acquaintance of this anecdote as evidence of something being demonstrated by a detail, of representation by something very small. It is meant to portray the democratic mode of thinking of Jews, which recognizes no distinction between lords and serfs, but also, alas, upsets discipline and co-operation.

Freud recognizes the fact that when Jews poke "fun" at themselves, it has a light and essentially egalitarian, freeing quality; it is not a sign of Jews being masochistic and turning the hatred they found around them into masochistic humor. The editor and translator of Freud's book on humor also adds an important point in a footnote:

> [Displacement on to something very small was later recognized by Freud as a characteristic mechanism in obsessional neurosis. See the "Rat Man" case history. . . .]

This point and Freud's comment about Jews making fun of themselves have been used by those who argue the thesis that Jewish humor is essentially masochistic.

Martin Grotjahn, a Freudian psychiatrist who was not Jewish, offers his interpretation of Jewish humor and its relation to masochism in *Beyond Laughter: Humor and the Subconscious.* In this book he writes (1966, 22):

> The Jewish joke is only a masochistic mask; it is by no means a sign of masochistic perversion. The Jewish joke constitutes victory by defeat. The persecuted Jew who makes himself the butt of the joke deflects his dangerous hostility away from the persecutors onto himself. The result is not defeat or surrender but victory and greatness.

Grotjahn is defending Jewish humor, but even this notion that Jewish humor is a masochistic mask strikes me as a mistake. I don't see the masochism in people making fun of themselves or being critical of themselves, but see these phenomena as being, instead, liberating and life-enhancing. The notion that being critical of oneself is equivalent to being a masochist strikes me as much too simplistic.

Let me offer a joke, in which Jews poke fun of themselves, that deals with the main branches of Judaism (Orthodox, Conservative, Reform, and Reconstructionist) in a humorous way.

Who's Pregnant
When you go to an Orthodox wedding, the mother of the bride is pregnant. When you go to a Conservative wedding, the bride is pregnant. When you go to a Reform wedding, the rabbi is pregnant. And when you go to a Reconstructionist wedding, both brides are pregnant—by artificial insemination.

This joke pokes fun at the different kinds of Jews, brides, and rabbis one finds in contemporary American society, but it certainly is not a sign of masochism or any kind of morbidity. There is a considerable difference, I would argue, between a person feeling "up" at times and "down" at other times and being a manic-depressive, bipolar personality. The same applies to poking fun at oneself and being a masochist.

From time to time, when people make a stupid mistake, they say "sometimes I think I'm my own worst enemy." Is that a revelation of some self-destructive form of unconscious masochism? I'm reminded of Groucho Marx's wonderful comment when he heard someone say, to himself,

> *"Sometimes I think I'm my own worst enemy!"*
> *Groucho Marx replied: "Not while I'm alive!"*

Freud made a point about the liberating nature of humor and the way it shields people from pain in his essay "Humour," in which he writes (Rieff, ed., *Freud: Character and Culture*, 1963, 265):

> Like wit and the comic, humour has in it a *liberating* element. But it has also something fine and elevating, which is lacking in the other two ways of deriving pleasure from intellectual activity. Obviously, what is fine about it is the triumph of narcissism, the ego's victorious assertion of its own invulnerability. It refuses to be hurt by the arrows of reality or to be compelled to suffer. It insists that it is impervious to wounds dealt by the outside world, in fact, that these are merely occasions for affording it pleasure.

These words do not suggest that humor, and in particular Jewish jokes, are signs of masochism, by any means. Humor, Freud suggests a bit later in the essay, is a means to ward off suffering and to uphold the pleasure principle.

Theodore Reik has also found a connection between Jewish humor and masochism (and paranoid feelings, as well). He distinguishes between masochistic and paranoid traits (*Jewish Wit*, 1962, 227):

> The masochistic character is over critical of himself, sees his own person as weak, insignificant, despicable and dependent. He degrades and humiliates himself with others, while the paranoid character behaves haughtily and sees mostly negative features in others. The masochistic character often punishes himself or provokes punishment by another, while the paranoid character, assuming that he will be the subject of hostility, forestalls the attack of his real or imagined enemies and degrades and offends them.

Reik also points out that masochism and paranoia are connected and that there is often paranoia concealed behind masochism. This leads him to suggest (1962, 228):

> It is difficult to put the Jewish jokes into one of the pigeon holes which comparative psychology has established. The great number of jokes we quoted and their survey will be sufficient to justify the statement that the Jewish jokes oscillate between an ingratiating and a provocative attitude and they move back and forth between a masochistic and a paranoid behavior-pattern. The paranoid attitude is certainly, in most cases, latent or hidden.

Reik has got everyone coming and going: if a joke isn't masochistic, it most likely reflects a latent paranoia hidden behind the masochism. And if a joke reflects a paranoid sensibility, it is inevitably a mask for a latent masochism. The two are, he informs us, opposite and complementary.

Consider the following joke Jews make about a rabbi's behavior during their most sacred holiday—Yom Kippur, the Day of Atonement.

The Rabbi Who Ate Oysters

A member of a congregation is driving by a restaurant, on his way back home during a break in the Yom Kippur services, and thinks he sees his rabbi in a restaurant eating oysters. The next year the congregation hires a private detective to trail the rabbi during the Yom Kippur period, and sure enough, during the break, the rabbi goes to a restaurant and has a big plate of oysters. The next week the board of the congregation confronts the rabbi with the private detective. "I trailed the rabbi and he had a big plate of oysters during the break in the Yom Kippur services," says the detective. "But doesn't September have an 'R' in it?" asks the rabbi.

We must keep in mind that Jews are supposed to fast during Yom Kippur and that oysters and all other shellfish are *traif*, that is, not Kosher and not supposed to be eaten by Jews. When the rabbi says that September has an "R" in it, and therefore one can eat oysters, he is displacing the criticism the same way the person in the salmon and mayonnaise joke, recounted earlier, did.

The rabbi shouldn't eat during Yom Kippur, and he most certainly shouldn't eat oysters, but he counters the revelation he did with the "rule" that one can eat oysters in months in which there is an "R." In this joke, we can see a sense of realism that Jews have about the temptations and allure of that which is not allowed, when even a rabbi is not able to withstand temptation. If rabbis eat during Yom Kippur—and eat oysters, which is even worse—we can sympathize with ordinary Jews who may exhibit this or that failing and succumb to this or that temptation. This joke humanizes rabbis and recognizes that rabbis can be as weak as anyone else. Is this the masochism that Reik sees in Jewish jokes, even as he tries to defend Jews against the notion that Jewish jokes are masochistic? Jewish jokes, he tells us, only *seem* masochistic. I most certainly would not agree.

Harvey Mindess argues, in *Laughter and Liberation*, that Jewish jokes that poke fun at Jews and Judaism are not signs of masochism. As he writes (1971, 49):

> Is the Jew who makes fun of his idiosyncrasies a masochist? Is he motivated, as some so-called experts have claimed, by a need to feel humiliated? Nonsense! Jewish laughter at jests . . . is evidence not of masochism but of expanded perspective, of what D.H. Monro has called the "god's eye view." It is evidence of rising above one's deficiencies by frankly admitting them and enjoying them.

Mindess suggests that these Jewish jokes recognize the absurdity of life, the injustice we find in human affairs, and enable Jews to become free and detached observers of their fate. Rather than being signs of masochism, these self-critical Jewish jokes are signifiers of a sense of liberation and freedom.

REIK ON JEWS AS SCHLEMIELS

Reik also suggests that the Jewish people can be seen as schlemiels, who are by definition masochistic, with "a subterranean compulsion to repeat" their failures—that is, a will to fail. As he explains: "Psychoanalysis would characterize a Shlemihl as a masochistic character who has the strong unconscious will to fail and to spoil his chances . . . the Schlemihl is the hidden architect of his misfortune" (1962, 41). He points out that Gentiles as well as Jews are shlemiels, but Jewish shlemiels seem to have a will to fail.

Jews, he adds, "are the Shlemihls of history with a difference: they cling to the deathless hope that they will not always be vexed victims of a cruel fate, but will be finally vindicated victors" (1962, 42). If Jews as schlemiels are the architects of their own misfortune, how do you explain the incredible success Jews have had in America? Once it was possible for them to succeed (and anti-Semitism held them back, in many areas), the Jews seem to have cast off their "unconscious will to fail" and flourished to an extraordinary degree.

Reik's perspective suggests that being a schlemiel is a matter of choice, more or less, tied to individual personality problems, and totally disregards the social and political arrangements that existed in the shtetls and Eastern Europe that pushed individuals into becoming schlemiels, schnorrers, and so on, as a means of surviving. Saying that Jews are (as a people) schlemiels, blames the victim and disregards historical situations that oppressed many Jews. Reik did recognize the fact that the Jews were continually persecuted and segregated, which, he says, explains why Jews wandered so much. Eventually, he suggests, repetition compulsion took over the Jewish personality and many of the wanderings were voluntary. It wasn't external pressure that shaped the Jewish personality but something internal, a repetition compulsion.

I would suggest that Reik's views reflect a somewhat doctrinaire and simplistic psychoanalytic approach to Jewish jokes, one that interprets them in a paradigm of psychoanalytic theory that is somewhat narrow and confining, seeing everything in terms of neuroses and psychopathology. There is, in Reik's perspective—or perhaps we should put it more strongly, there *must* be—a psychopathological element buried in these jokes. While I am very sympathetic to psychoanalytic theory, I also believe that we must recognize the connection between a person's behavior and social, economic, and political matters.

A Jewish riddle belies the dark and somewhat depressing view of the Jewish personality we find in Reik.

Why Are Jews Optimists?
Q. Why are the Jews the most optimistic people in the world?
A. They cut half of it off before they know how long it's going to be.

This joke refers, of course, to the Jewish ritual of circumcision—a matter that is the subject of a number of Jewish jokes and gags. Reik suggests that because the Jews circumcise male children, non-Jews see them as dangerous castrating figures. But what about the Muslims and Christians who circumcise *their* male children?

Christie Davies offers some interesting ideas on this matter of self-critical Jewish jokes. He doesn't accept the notion that Jewish jokes are masochistic because he ties these jokes to the difficult social conditions and the oppression that Jews had to contend with. As he writes in *Ethnic Humor Around the World* (1990, 122):

> I am much more convinced by the argument of Ziv . . . that "self-disparaging" jokes told by Jews in the face of both external hostility and internal division are ways of

coping with a harsh reality by making it temporarily appear less threatening. Also, internal differentiation and division always allow ethnic jokes to be told about another section of the joke-teller's own group, one to which he or she does not belong.

Davies also mentions work by Victor Raskin on "scripts" for a significant number of Jewish jokes that show Jewish cleverness in a positive way (as some of the jokes told in this book do) that give us different perspectives on Jewish jokes and humor and suggest that the masochism thesis is simplistic and reductionistic.

It is useful to recognize that Jews are often stereotyped as critical, in general, not only of themselves but everyone else. This explains the following joke.

The Luncheon
Three upper-middle class Jewish American women go to a restaurant for lunch. A half hour after they are served, the waiter comes over and asks, "is anything *all right?*

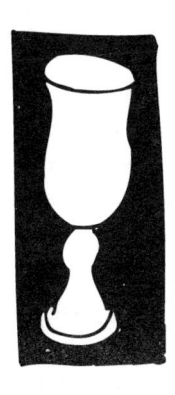

Here we have a sly reversal on the typical question waiters ask: "Is everything all right?" This joke alludes to the critical nature of Jewish women, and perhaps Jews in general, which may stem, in part, from the ethical aspects of Judaism. That is, the critical nature of Jewish behavior mocked in so many jokes is a secularization of the religio-ethical concept of Judaism applied to everyday life. It can be argued that the "self-critical" nature of some Jewish jokes, the tendency of Jews to "kvetch" (complain) about this and that, is grounded in Jewish ethical thought. That explains the joke about an old Jewish man on a bus who was continually complaining, "Oy, am I thirsty." After being given something to drink, he complained, "Oy *was* I thirsty."

ON EROSGOPANALIA AND IDI AMIN: TWO PERSONAL EXAMPLES

Let me offer a couple of examples of amusing things that have happened to me as a case in point. In the mid-seventies I published a book, *The TV-Guided American*. This was a period, I should point out, when Idi Amin was getting an enormous amount of coverage for killing huge numbers of people in Uganda. My book was reviewed by Jeff Greenfield in *The New York Times Book Review*. He was not favorably impressed by my use of psychoanalytic theory and semiotics and concluded his review with the following statement: "*Berger is to the study of television what Idi Amin is to tourism in Uganda!*" (My italics.)

My second example involves a bit of humor that evidently was not very successful. I wrote a zany article in which I suggested that conservative Republicans suffered from Anal Eroticism and had transferred their desire to hold in their stools to one in which they were unwilling to spend any money on welfare programs and other governmental programs (except for defense spending). I coined a term, ErosGOPanalia, and wrote an article, "ErosGOPanalia: The Berger Hypottythesis," in which I suggested that it was the toilet training of our congressmen and women and senators that really was responsible for their political and economic views. I even threw in a parody:

*The potty does more
Than Milton (Friedman) can
To justify the ways
Of the NAM to man!*

I sent this article to a very distinguished economics journal as a lark, and received a letter back from the editor that went as follows:

Dear Professor Berger:
 The editors of the journal would like to thank you for submitting your article, "ErosGOPanalia: The Berger Hypottythesis" to our journal for consideration. We have reviewed your article and are sorry to inform you that it is not suitable for publication in our journal . . . or any other journal that we can possibly conceive of.
 Sincerely yours,
 The Editor

Now when I give lectures, I often start them by telling about the review of my book in *The New York Times* and the rejection letter from the economics journal, and when I recount these tales, I get a great deal of laughter from my audiences.

Is my recounting the hostile line (which I think is really wonderful) suggesting a parallel between me and Idi Amin and the story of my rejection by the editors of an august economics journal, suggesting my article was not fit for any journal that could be conceived of, a study is masochistic self-flagellating behavior?
 Not at all. Just the opposite, in fact.

When I tell audiences about the Greenfield review and the journal's rejection letter, I use these comic "insults" as an opportunity for making fun of those who made them. When I tell the stories of these two criticisms, I give my audiences good reason to laugh at Jeff Greenfield and the board of editors of the economics journal. If you look at the two statements out of context and literally, without any sense of how I am using them, it looks like I am a masochist recounting tales about my "humiliations."

But that is not the case at all. I would like to suggest that many Jewish jokes that are self-critical function the same way. That is, Jews use self-critical jokes and jokes in which they make "fun" of themselves for purposes other than expressing their masochism, self-hatred, or whatever.

HUMOR AND THE JEWS

Elliott Oring has a number of hypotheses about Jewish humor in his book *Jokes and Their Relations* that are worth exploring. His first is that Jewish humor is relatively new (1992, 116): "<u>Jewish humor is a relatively modern invention. The conceptualization of humor that was in some way characteristic or distinctive of the Jewish people begins only in Europe during the nineteenth century.</u>" As evidence for this notion, he mentions that in 1893, the Chief Rabbi of London, Hermann Adler, had written that Jews "were a humourless people" (1992, 116). Oring adds that most of the Jewish humor we know comes from the twentieth century.

Reik offers other examples to support this "humorless" hypothesis. He mentions that Ernest Renan argued that Semitic people lack the facility to laugh and that Carlyle claimed that there is no period in Jewish history in which Jews showed they had a sense of humor. Reik argues that Renan and Carlyle were mistaken and didn't recognize that there could be suffering and humor at the same time.

If you accept my argument that there is humor in the Bible, then the arguments that there is no Jewish humor, or that Jewish humor started only in the twentieth century, become hard to accept. I find it difficult to imagine that a people without a developed sense of humor suddenly becomes an enormously humorous people. In addition, we know that in the Middle Ages there was a considerable amount of Jewish humor. In his book *National Styles of Humor,* Avner Ziv writes (1988, 115):

> Many references to laughter, humorous tales, and rules about joking appear in the Talmud. It seems that Talmudic sages were able to differentiate between "laughing at" and "laughing with." While formal prohibitions to laugh at are frequently mentioned, other views, where the accent is on "laughing with" are encouraged.

Laughing at would be hostile and aggressive humor, and laughing with would be sympathetic and affectionate humor, in today's terms.

Ziv also mentions that in the Middle Ages, during Purim, a Purim rabbi was selected for one day, whose behavior caricatured that of a real rabbi. This Purim rabbi gave illogical, nonsensical, and humorous "rabbinical decisions" and amused everyone. Purim, we must remember, is a holiday in which Jews celebrate their escape from annihilation by their Persian enemies thanks to Queen Esther's efforts. People are supposed to be merry and drink—even get drunk—so they cannot tell the difference between Haman (the villain) and Esther. (This Purim rabbi is probably a Jewish version of a Christian tradition in which a clown became priest and parodied Christian religious teachings. This topic is discussed by Bakhtin in some detail in his book on Rabelais.) It is reasonable to argue that the Jews have been a humorous people for many centuries and did not develop a sense of humor in the nineteenth century.

Oring has a second hypothesis, one which he argues is "little more than a suspicion," to explain his first hypothesis. As he writes (1992, 117): "Toward the end of the nineteenth century, the faculty of humor was felt to be one of the signs of a civilized humanity, and Jews felt the necessity to demonstrate that they had participated in this humanity since their emergence as a people." According to this argument, the humorless Jews decided to show the Gentiles that they were "civilized" and thus developed, somehow, a sense of humor—out of the blue, so to speak. Jews would show people that they did not spent all of their time in arcane and legalistic disputes over the Torah, but had a "human" side.

As evidence for this suspicion, he mentions a book, *Sex and Character*, published in 1903 by a Jewish anti-Semite, Otto Weininger. Weininger argued that humor had a transcendental quality to it and was tolerant, while wit and satire were intolerant. Oring quotes Weininger, "Jews and women are devoid of humour, but addicted to mockery." The argument then turns to how one defines humor and becomes, I would say, insupportable. Opinions vary about what humor is and isn't. If wit and satire are not humor, what are they? I realize it is possible to make distinctions between wit, satire, the comic, comedy, and other related forms, but all of them fall, I would suggest, under the general category of humor.

I accept Ziv's definition of humor (1988, ix):

> *Humor* is therefore defined as a social message intended to produce laughter or smiling. As with any social message, it fulfills certain functions, uses certain techniques, has a content, and is used in certain situations. These aspects of humor can be understood as relating to the questions of *why* people use humor (its functions), *how* it is transmitted (techniques), *what* it communicates (content), and *where and when* it is communicated (situation). Some of these aspects are universal, characterizing humor everywhere. Others are more influenced by culture.

Ziv points out that there are no differences in the techniques used in humor, so we must look at the functions of humor when we analyze it. I have suggested earlier that Jewish humor tends to use certain techniques and not use others due, in great measure, to the social situation of living in the shtetls and cultural arrangements that developed in response to this social situation.

Oring has several other hypotheses to offer in his book, dealing with the conceptualization of Jewish history as that of suffering, which suggests that Jewish humor is different from other kinds of humor that are not tied to despair. This leads to his final hypothesis (1992, 118-119):

> <u>If the background of Jewish suffering did condition the expectation of a distinctive Jewish humor, there was only a limited range of possibilities for articulating this history of suffering with humor. The possibilities were that humor</u>

<u>was</u> "transcendent," <u>that the humor was</u> "defensive," <u>or that the humor was</u> "pathological."

Each of these possibilities, he continues, suggests reasons why Jews should laugh.

I have already dealt with these notions in this book. The first view, that humor can be "transcendent," is found in my discussion of the optimism of the Jews and their ability to function in a world where they were relatively weak and powerless. Humor made it possible for Jews to survive in impossible conditions. The second notion, that humor is "defensive," involves the notion that Jewish humor helped shield Jews from pain and was a method of using their hostility in ways that were often not recognized, and a way of rebelling against oppressive forces both outside and inside the Jewish community. The third notion suggests that Jewish humor is masochistic and, in Reik's views, that Jews are quintessential schlemiel figures who unconsciously want to fail (though I may be oversimplifying his views a bit).

SOME DISTINCTIVE ASPECTS OF JEWISH HUMOR

Christie Davies, in a fascinating article titled "An Explanation of Jewish Jokes About Jewish Women," focuses his attention on two important themes in Jewish jokes about Jewish men and one key theme that is absent in Jewish jokes. He points out that many jokes about Jewish males focus upon the first key theme, which has to do with (*Humor,* vol. 3-4, 368) the problematic boundary of the Jewish people who have survived centuries in exile by upholding a distinctive code of ritual and moral behavior that emphasizes both directly and metaphorically their separate and special status. . . . There are *far* more Jewish jokes about the perils and temptations of assimilation, or apostasy, about rule and boundary breaking and about imitation of and masquerading as members of another group than is the case with any other ethnic group.

So Jewish jokes are unique in that they reflect a terrible anxiety about Jews assimilating and, ultimately, of Judaism, as we now know it, disappearing. Marrying a Jewish girl becomes a kind of moral duty for Jewish men—one that Jewish men have rebelled against in increasing numbers in recent decades, as they have succumbed to the temptations of marrying shiksas.

Let me offer a joke that deals with this theme.

Sitting Shivah

A young Jewish girl goes off to college in Oklahoma. In her senior year she meets a handsome Native American and falls in love with him and he falls in love with her and they decide to get married. So she calls her parents and tells them what has happened and asks them to come to Oklahoma to meet her fiancé and his parents. The parents take a plane to Oklahoma. When they land they are picked up in a van and are brought to an Indian reservation. They are ushered into a huge teepee, where their daughter and her fiancé are waiting for them. A big tall Indian, wearing a set of feathers, comes forward and introduces himself. "I'm Chief Sitting Bull," he says. He points to a woman and says, "And this is my wife, Sitting Fawn." He points to their daughter's fiancé and says, "And this is my son, Sitting Bear. What is your name?" he asks. "I'm sitting shivah," says the girl's mother.

Sitting *shivah*, we must remember, is a ceremony performed for the dead, in which relatives of a dead person spend a week at home, mourning. When the mother says she's "sitting *shivah*," a play on words, she's saying that as far as she's concerned, her daughter is dead. This alludes to a practice of some Orthodox Jews of "sitting *shivah*" when their children marry outside of the Jewish religion. In contemporary American society, as I mentioned earlier, the rate of intermarriage between Jews and non-Jews has reached approximately 50 percent, so having a son or daughter marry "out" is not as shocking as it was twenty or thirty years ago.

The second theme Christie notices in his study of Jewish jokes about Jewish males has to do with the absence of violence. As he writes (1990, 369): "A second theme in Jewish humor about Jewish males that is striking to an outsider is 'restraint,' that is, self-control over aggression which is by inference contrasted with the brawling and hooliganism of the Gentiles." So the second theme Christie finds is that Jewish men tend to avoid violence or using violence as a means of attaining some goal or end. There are many jokes about *schvartzes* (Blacks) in Jewish neighborhoods getting mugged by accountants or being worried because they see four accountants walking down the block, and so on. These are reversals of jokes Jews tell about being mugged or attacked by Blacks . . . or being afraid of being attacked by them.

Two Jews Who See Two Schvartses
Two Jews are walking down the street when they see two blacks. "Let's get out of here," says one of the Jews. "There are two of them and we're here all by ourselves."

This joke deals with the stereotypes of Blacks, or in Yiddish, *schvartzes*, as being violent. Ziv points out in his book on national styles of humor that Israeli jokes also don't deal with drinking or violence.

The third theme Christie considers important is that Jewish jokes about men also show a remarkable paucity of jokes about getting drunk. He is struck by the relative absence of jokes about Jewish men getting drunk, while there are endless numbers of jokes about male Irish, Finns, Germans, Australians, and Scots getting drunk. These jokes, Christie points out, are connected to socioeconomic matters. Each of these drinking ethnicities were connected to working conditions in which they were isolated, and each developed an "all-male, hard-drinking bachelor culture." Let me offer a typical drinking joke here.

Two Finns Decide to Go Drinking
Two Finns decide to go drinking. They sit without saying a word to each other for hours, drinking. After drinking for a whole day, one of the Finns raises his glass of beer and says "Skol!" The other Finn looks at him. "Did we come here to talk or to drink?" he asks.

Christie concludes that Jewish jokes about men show them as deeply enmeshed in family life, without time for drinking. They are also, he says, portrayed as diligent, nonviolent homebodies and, as such, good catches. It is reasonable to suggest that many Gentile women recognize this and may be attracted to, or even seek out, Jewish men for these reasons.

He concludes with an explanation of why Jewish men make the jokes they do about Jewish women (1990, 375):

> Once again, the Jewish sense of family duty has prevailed over temptation, and the inevitable result is jokes that mock the moral guardians of the Jewish world—Jewish mothers and present and future wives. Far from being an index of misogyny and patriarchy, Jewish jokes about women . . . are a wry acknowledgment of the powerful and legitimized influence that Jewish women exercise, especially when contrasted with women-folk of other ethnic communities.

This would suggest that all the jokes about Jewish mothers and Jewish American Princesses are not what they may seem at first sight—harsh attacks on Jewish mothers and "spoiled" Jewish women—but rather playful responses by Jewish men to the authority and power of Jewish women.

CONCLUSIONS

Jewish humor is so vibrant, so rich, so complicated, that it is impossible to cover every aspect of it. I have limited myself, in this book, to Jewish jokes—though I would suggest that this discussion of Jewish jokes is also a discussion of Jewish humor in general. There is an enormous literature on Jewish humor, and I've used some of the more interesting theories and concepts by a wide variety of writers to explicate Jewish jokes.

I've used a large number of jokes. I'm not sure whether this book is a joke book with fillers about Judaism, Jewish humor, and so on, or a book on Jewish jokes and humor with a goodly sampling of Jewish (and some non-Jewish) jokes. Whatever the case, I hope you have learned something about the Jewish joke and about Jews, and in learning about Jewish jokes and Jews, learned something about what might be described as "the human condition." In this respect, let me conclude with a joke that is found in Freud's book on jokes and is relevant—it finishes off the Jews and everyone else very nicely.

On Not Being Born

Two Jewish philosophers are talking. "Never to be born would be the best thing for mortal men," says one.

"Yes," says the other, "but that happens to scarcely one person in a hundred thousand!"

Glossary of Yiddish Terms

Babeh Grandmother, old woman
Bar Mitzvah Confirmation for thirteen-year-old boys
Bat Mitzvah Confirmation for thirteen-year-old girls
Boichik Boy (*chick* is an affectionate suffix)
Bubele General purpose term for affection (from *boba*)
Challah A Jewish egg bread
Chelm A town of fools
Fresser Eater—someone who is often eating
Gelt Money
Goniff Robber, thief (often has an affectionate tone to it)
Goy A Gentile
JAP Jewish American Princess
Jewish Mother Overly solicitous character who, according to the stereotype, focuses all her attention on feeding her children, having sons who are doctors, and marrying daughters off to doctors or lawyers

Kibitzer A joker or teaser; someone who comments on what is going on
Kiddush An original synthesis based on the study of the Talmud
Kosher Food that can be eaten by observant Jews
Kvetch Complain
Luftmensch A person who "lives on air," gets by on nothing
Matzos Unleavened bread eaten by Jews during Passover
Maven Expert, someone really good at something
Mazel Tov Congratulations
Megillah The whole thing . . . a long story . . . the term for the escape from the Egyptians told during the Passover seder
Mensch A decent person
Meshugeh Crazy, mad, insane. We say "he's meshugah" or "he's a meshugeneh"
Mohel Person who circumsizes male babies
Momser Bastard, no-goodnik
Naches Pleasure
Nosh Snack
Nu? Well? So?
Pilpul "Pepper." Intellectual analysis of the Torah carried on by Jews in yeshivas
Purim Festive Jewish holiday celebrating triumph of Jews over Haman
Schlemiel Clutzy simpleton. Always spilling soup
Schlimazel Person with bad luck. When a schlemiel spills soup, he spills it on a schlimazel. A born loser
Schmendrik A weak, thin, pip-squeak
Schmeggege A maladroit, whining, petty person

Glossary of Yiddish Terms

Schmuck A jerk. (The term also means penis)
Schnorrer A professional beggar, who made it possible for wealthy Jews to give alms and discharge their duties toward the poor
Seder A ritual meal, at the beginning of the Passover period, which progresses in a certain order, that celebrates the escape of the Jews from Egypt. The term *seder* means order
Shadken A marriage broker who always has to convince Jewish men to marry deaf, blind, ugly, stupid, hunchbacked, etc., women
Shammas A non-Jew who works at synagogues and turns lights off and on and does other chores
Shaygits Non-Jewish boy or man
Shiksa Non-Jewish girl or woman
Shlep Carry, bring, pull
Shloomp A drag, a drip, a wet blanket
Shnook A timid, weak soul
Shtetl Small Jewish town in Eastern Europe
Shvartze A black person
Sit Shivah Week of remembrance for the dead
Talmud Multivolume compilation of Jewish Law consisting of the Mishnah and the Gemorrah
Torah The first five books of the Old Testament
Tsuris Trouble, problems, difficulties
Vay is mir Woe unto me. Often preceded by an "Oy"
Yeshivah Place of learning, where the Talmud and commentators on the Talmud are studied.
Yiddish Dialect spoken by Jews based on German
Yom Kippur Holiest holiday of the Jews, marked by a fast
Zaftig Juicy, well built (used for women)

Bibliography

BOOKS

Ausubel, Nathan, ed. *A Treasury of Jewish Folklore.* New York: Crown Publishers, 1978.

Berger, Arthur Asa. *Li'l Abner: A Study in American Satire.* New York: Twayne Publishers, 1970.

———, ed. *American Behavioral Scientist* issue on "Humor, The Psyche, and Society." Jan./Feb. 1987. Thousand Oaks, CA: Sage Publications.

———. *An Anatomy of Humor.* New Brunswick, NJ: Transaction Publishers, 1993.

———. *Blind Men and Elephants: Perspectives on Humor.* New Brunswick, NJ: Transaction Publishers, 1995.

Cohen, Sarah, ed. *Jewish Wry.* Bloomington, IN: Indiana University Press, 1987.

Davies, Christie. *Ethnic Humor Around the World.* Bloomington, IN: Indiana University Press, 1990.

Douglas, Mary. *Implicit Meanings: Essays in Anthropology*. London: Routledge & Kegan Paul, 1975.

Dundes, Alan. *Cracking Jokes: Studies of Sick Humor Cycles and Stereotypes*. Berkeley, CA: Ten Speed Press, 1987.

Freud, Sigmund (trans. James Strachey). *Jokes and Their Relation to the Unconscious*. New York: Norton, 1963.

Fry, William. *Sweet Madness: A Study of Humor*. Palo Alto, CA: Pacific Books, 1963.

Harris, David, and Izrail Rachmiah. *The Jews of Oppression: The Humor of Soviet Jews*. Northvale, NJ: Jason Aronson, 1988.

Mindess, Harvey. *Laughter and Liberation*. Los Angeles: Nash Publishing Co., 1971.

Novak, William, and Moshe Waldoks, eds. *The Big Book of Jewish Humor*. New York: Harper & Row, 1981.

Oring, Elliott. *Jokes of Sigmund Freud*. Philadelphia, PA: University of Pennsylvania Press, 1984.

Pinsker, Sanford. *The Schlemiel as a Metaphor: Studies in the Yiddish and American Jewish Novel*. Carbondale, IL: Southern Illinois University Press, 1971.

Powell, Chris, and George E. C. Paton, eds. *Humor in Society: Resistance and Control*. New York: St. Martin's Press, 1988.

Raskin, Richard. *Life Is Like a Glass of Tea: Studies of Classic Jewish Jokes*. Aarhus, DK: Aarhus University Press, 1992.

Raskin, Victor. *Semantic Mechanisms of Humor*. Dordecht: D. Reidel, 1985.

Reiff, Philip, ed. *Sigmund Freud: Character and Culture*. New York: Collier Books, 1963.

Reik, Theodore. *Jewish Wit*. New York: Gamut Press, 1962.

Rosten, Leo. *The Joys of Yiddish.* New York: Penguin Books, 1968.
Saussure, Ferdinand de (trans. Wade Baskin). *Course in General Linguistics.* New York: McGraw-Hill Book Co., 1966.
Sypher, Wylie, ed. *Comedy.* Garden City, NY: Doubleday Anchor Books, 1956.
Wisse, Ruth R. *The Schlemiel as Modern Hero.* Chicago: University of Chicago Press, 1971.
Zborowski, Mark, and Elizabeth Herzog. *Life Is With People: The Culture of the Shtetl.* New York: Schocken Books, 1952.
Ziv, Avner, ed. *Jewish Humor.* Tel Aviv: Papyrus/Tel Aviv University, 1986.
——. *National Styles of Humor.* New York: Greenwood Press, 1988.

ARTICLES

Apte, Mahadav L. "Ethnic Humor Versus 'Sense of Humor.'" *American Behavioral Scientist*, vol. 30, no. 3 (Jan./Feb.1987): 27-41.
Ben-Amos, Dan. "The Myth of Jewish Humor." *Western Folklore* 32 (1973): 113-31.
Bennett, D. J. "The Psychological Meaning of Anti-Negro Jokes." *Fact* (March-April 1964): 53-59.
Benton, Gregor. "The Origins of the Political Joke." In *Humor in Society: Resistance and Control.* Ed. Chris Powell and George E. C. Paton (New York: St. Martin's Press, 1988): 33-55.
Brandes, Stanley. "Jewish-American Dialect Jokes and Jewish-American Identity." *Jewish Social Studies* XLV 3-4 (Summer-Fall, 1983): 233-40.

Davies, Christie. "An Explanation of Jewish Jokes About Jewish Women." *Humor*, vol. 3-4 (1990): 363-78.

Dundes, Alan. "Many Hands Make Light Work or Caught in the Act of Screwing in Light Bulbs." *Western Folklore* 40 (1981): 261-66.

Dundes, Alan, and Roger Abrahams. "On Elephantasy and Elephanticide." *The Psychoanalytic Review* 56:2 (1969): 225-41.

Ornstein-Galicia, Jacob L. "Dem Kibbizers Maven: Yiddish Language Contact and Affective Borrowing." Unpublished Paper, undated.

Spencer, Gary. "An Analysis of JAP-Baiting Humor on the College Campus." *Humor* 2:4 (1989): 329-48.

Wildavsky, Aaron. "Conditions for Pluralist Democracy or Pluralism Means More than One Political Culture in a Country." Unpublished paper. Survey Research Center, University of California, Berkeley. *See also* **Arthur Asa Berger, *Agitpop: Political Culture and Communication Theory.* New Brunswick, NJ: Transaction Publishers, 1990.**

Ziv, Avner. "Introduction." *Humor*, vol. 4-2 (1991): 145-48.

Index of Names

Abrahams, Roger, 123, 132
Adler, Hermann, 150
Aleichem, Shalom, 11
Allen, Woody, xi, 11, 19
Amin, Idi, 149
Apte, Mahadev L., 135
Aristophanes, xi
Aristotle, xi, 92
Ausubel, Nathan, 83, 104, 105

Bennett, D. J., 51, 52, 53, 55
Benny, Jack, 19
Benton, Gregor, 37, 38, 41
Berger, Arthur Asa, 42, 43, 135, 136, 148, 149
Bergson, Henri, xi, 85, 86, 91
Boone, Pat, 113
Brandes, Stanley, 87, 88

Caesar, Sid, 19
Capp, Al, 97, 98
Carlyle, Thomas, 151
Clay, Andrew Dice, 19

Index of Names

D'Amato, Al, 65
Darwin, Charles, 3
Davies, Christie, 50, 64, 67, 68, 130, 131, 146, 147, 154, 156, 157
Descartes, Rene, 3
Douglas, Mary, 26, 27
Dundes, Alan, 32, 112, 113, 119, 123, 124, 129, 132

Einstein, Albert, xiv
Ezra, Abraham ibn, 99

Freud, Sigmund, xi, 3, 76, 101, 102, 111, 112, 138, 139, 141
Fry, William, 91

Graham, Billy, 113
Greenfield, Jeff, 148
Grotjahn, Manin, 136, 139, 140

Hegel, Georg Wilhelm Friedrich, 3
Herzog, Elizabeth, 16, 106

Ionesco, Eugene, xi, 73

Jonson, Ben, xi

Kant, Immanuel, xi

Lenin, Nikolai, 39
Locke, John, 3

Marx, Groucho, 141
Mindess, Harvey, 144

Oring, Elliott, 150, 152
Ornstein-Galicia, Jacob L., 40, 89, 90, 91
Orwell, George, 46

Paton, George E. C., 38
Piddington, Ralph, 3
Plautus, xi
Powell, Chris, 38
Propp, Vladimir, 80

Raskin, Richard, 112
Raskin, Victor, 48, 147
Reiff, Philip, 141
Reik, Theodore, 141, 142, 144, 145, 146, 154
Renan, Ernest, 150, 151
Rosten, Leo, 93, 97, 98, 105
Rousseau, Jean Jacques, 3
Ruth, Babe, 117

Saussure, Ferdinand de, 67
Schopenhauer, Arthur, 3
Shakespeare, William, xi
Simon, Neil, xi, 11
Socrates, 66, 133

Index of Names

Spencer, Gary, 70, 71
Spencer, Herbert, 3
Stalin, Joseph, 39, 90
Stoppard, Tom, xi
Sypher, Wylie, 86

Trotsky, Leon, 39, 90

Weber, Max, 64
Weininger, Otto, 152

Wildavsky, Aaron, 42
Wilde, Oscar, xi
Wisse, Ruth R., 92, 94, 95, 98

Zborowski, Mark, 16, 106
Ziv, Avner, 11, 12, 13, 14, 36, 153

Index of Topics

Absurdity, 75–77
African-Americans. *See* Anti-Negro jokes
American humor
   yiddishization of, 36
Anti-Negro jokes, 51–56
Anti-Semitism, 18, 19, 37, 50, 81, 112, 115, 134
   jokes about Jews made by non-Jews, 112

Assimilation, 13, 19–21, 87, 88, 110, 119, 122, 134, 155, 156
   Jewish accents and, 87, 88, 119

Bulvans, 98

Chelm, 29, 71–73
   town of fools, 29
Comedy
   Aristotelian definition of, 92

Comedy (*continued*)
    superiority theory of humor and, 92

Dialect
    definition of, 91
    establishing play frame, 91
    use of in Jewish jokes, 87-92
Discrepant awareness, 73, 74

Eccentrics
    definition of, 85
    stratification and, 85
Elephant jokes
    as disguised anti-Negro jokes, 123-125
    Oedipal aspects of, 124
ErosGOPanalia satire
    Berger hypotythesis, 148, 149
    relation to masochism, 148, 149
Ethnic humor, 35, 111-136
    core American values and, 135
    stereotypes of Jews in, 112-120

Humor
    ah aspect of, 6
    ahah aspect of, 6
    chart of categories and techniques of, 4
    chart of techniques in alphabetical order, 56
    cognitive theory of, 4
    dominant theories of, 3-5
    enigmatic nature of, xi, xii
    ethnic, 35, 111-136
    haha aspect of, 6
    incongruity theory of, 3
    psychoanalytic theory of, 4
    superiority theory of, 3
    three ways to look at, 6
    tool for criticizing society, 20
    Ziv's definition of, 153

Ignorance, 71-74
Irony, 66, 67

Jewish American mother jokes, 68-71, 158
Jewish American Princess jokes, 69-71, 158

Index of Topics

Jewish humor. *See* Jewish jokes
   about kinds of congregations in America, 108-110
   absurd characters in, 83, 84
   as modern invention, 150-152
   definition of according to Avner Ziv, 11
   dialect usage in, 19, 20
   distinguishing characteristics of, 10-20
   egalitarian nature of, 84
   emotional aspects of, 14
   found in Torah, 32-35
   immigrant humor in America, 18
   intellectual dimension, 13
   Jewish identity and, 20-23
   limitations of hypothesis, 153, 154
   loss of Jewish identity and, 110
   new world, 24
   old world, 24
   problem of assimilation and, 13, 19, 110
   question of masochism in, 24, 137-144
   radical explanation of why Jews are so humorous, 32-35
   reflection of Jewish mentality, 24
   relations to humor in general, 14
   religious content of, 23
   shows Jews "civilized" hypothesis, 152
   social dimensions of, 13, 14
   subjects of, 23
   survival function of, 20
   use of types in, 85, 86
   victim humor, 50, 53
   Yeshivas importance for, 15-18

Jewish identity
   dialect in jokes and, 88, 89
   Jewish humor and, 20-23

Jewish jokes. *See* Jewish humor
   absence of violence in, 156, 157

Jewish jokes (*continued*)
   anxieties about assimilation and, 87, 88, 155, 156
   body language and, 90
   categories of, 35, 36
   distinctive aspects of, 154–158
   dynamics of, 136
   few jokes about getting drunk, 157
   functions of, xiii, 47–51
   genius of, xii
   Jewish humor and, xiv, xv
   liberating aspects of, 144
   new world, 49
   old world, 49
   phonological loans in, 40, 41
   political cultures and, 42–46
   rhetorical devices used in, 90, 91
   source of political jokes, 37–39
   stress on family duty, 158
   techniques of humor used in, 3
   use of dialect in, 87–92
Jewish mothers, 68–71, 75, 76

Jews
   as a people, 9, 10
   as chosen people, 25
   assimilation and loss of Jewish identity, 20–23, 87, 118
   Conservative congregations, 8, 9, 20, 109
   descend from ancient Hebrews, 9
   ethnic group, 10
   identify with Israel, 10
   intermarriage rate in America, 20
   Orthodox congregations, 8, 9, 20, 108, 100
   practice of Judaism, 8
   Reform congregations, 8, 9, 20, 109
   Reik on Jews as schlemiels, 144–146
   social marginality of, 81
   stereotypes of, 22, 23, 112–120
   who is Jewish?, 8–10
   why such a sense of humor, 5
Jokes
   anti-Negro, 51–56
   anti-Semitic, 134

Index of Topics

as performances, 30
difference from riddles, 29
elephant, 123-125
importance of punch lines, 26
insulting nature of, xvi
Italian-American, 121-123
light bulb, 127-129
national character formula, 129, 130
only one form of humor, 30
perspectives on, 80
play frames and, 56, 91
Polish, 125-127
relations to societies in which told, 26-28
relation to riddles 26
structure of, 28, 29
Tan joke analysis, 58, 60-63
technical definition of, 25, 26
told by Italian-Americans about themselves, 121-123
using techniques to reduce to a formula, 56-58

Kabala, 16
Khiddush, 16, 17
Kuni lemmels, 98
Kvetch, 148

Light bulb jokes, 127-129

Manischevitz matzos, xv, xvi
Masochism
  definition of, 137
  Freud's comment on Jewish humor, 138, 139
  Jewish humor and, 24
  Jewish jokes and, 137-144
  jokes about African-Americans and, 51-56
  mask of in Jewish jokes, 140
  paranoid traits and, 142
Matzos, 2, 77
Mistakes, 75
Misunderstanding, 78-80

National character jokes, 129, 130
Nebechs, 93

Paskudnyaks, 98
Paranoia
   relation to masochism, 141–144
Passover Seder, 1, 2
Pilpul, 16, 32
Play frames
   indicating humor, 91
   use of in anti-Negro jokes, 56
Political cultures
   competitive individualists, 43
   egalitarians, 43
   fatalists, 43
   hierarchical collectivists, 43
   Jewish jokes and, 42–46
Power
   techniques used by weak and powerless, 63–81
   use of humorous techniques and, 63–81
Psychoanalytic theory, 4, 37, 111, 112, 124, 125, 137–150
   elephant jokes and, 124, 125
   explanation of Jewish sense of humor, 37
   masochism hypothesis about Jewish humor, 137–150

Repartee, 76
Riddles, 26
   contest aspect of, 131
   definition of, 131
   difference from jokes, 29
   regressive nature of, 132
Rigidity, 85

Schlemiels, xv, 40, 83, 92–97
   basic attributes of, 93
   functions of, 94
   Jewish version of the fool, 92, 93
Schlimazels, xv, 40, 83, 97–101, 155
   Abraham ibn Ezra, 99
   born losers, 97
Schnorrers, 83, 98, 104–108
   connection to Jewish ethic of responsibility, 106
   connection to Jewish marginality, 105
Schvartses, 156, 157
Schadkens, 83, 101–104
   definition of, 101
   optimism of Jews and, 104

Index of Topics

  symbolic significance of, 103, 104
Shammas, 43-45
Shiksas, 21
Shivah, 156
Shloomps, 98
Shmeggeges, 98
Shmendriks, 98
Shmucks, 40, 98
Shnuks (or Shnooks), 40, 98
Shtetls, 24, 84, 86, 87, 106
Stereotypes, 56, 67-71, 129, 147
  African-Americans, 23
  Blacks as ignorant, 52
  defined, 50
  dominant kinds in ethnic humor, 68
  Indians as drunken and lazy, 52
  Italians as cowards, 50, 122
  Jews as cheap, 50
  Jews in jokes about Jews, 133, 134
  Jews in jokes by non-Jews, 112-118, 113-120
  national character and, 129, 130
  Poles in Polish jokes, 125-127
  Poles as dumb, 50
  relation to truth, 52
  role in ethnic humor, 50
  Scots as thrifty and canny, 120

Tan joke
  cognitive theorist analysis of, 61, 62
  feminist theorist analysis of, 62
  incongruity theorist analysis of, 60
  political analysis of, 62
  psychoanalytic analysis of, 60, 61
  superiority theorist analysis of, 60
  techniques of humor used in, 57, 58
  theories of humor and, 57-63
Techniques of humor
  concern with what makes us laugh, 4, 5
  use in analyzing Tan joke, 56-58
Torah, 32, 37, 45, 46, 96

Unmasking and revelation, 74, 75

Yeshivas
   importance for Jewish humor, 15–18
Yiddish, 16, 48, 87–91, 94, 95, 98
   dialect in Jewish jokes, 87–91
   different ways of spelling terms, xv
   humor, 95
   use of by Americans, 89
Yiddishization, 81
Yolds, 98
Yom Kippur, 66, 143, 144

Index of Jokes

Abbot visited by his mother, 12, 13
Absentminded scholar, 96, 97
Accident in Edinburgh, 120
A minor fault, 102
A Protestant, a Negro, and a Jew die . . . , 114
A woman with one fault, 101

Babe Ruth's Sixtieth Homerun, 117
Battle of Tannenberg, 95
Boss, 96
Bread and challah, 107
Buttered bread problem, 72
By a captain are you a captain? xiii

Census in Israel, 113
Clinic for the schnorrer, 107
Comedian who couldn't tell jokes, 59

Convert, 118
Convert's dilemma, 22

Denominationitis, 108, 109
Don't cause trouble, 51
Do you speak Yiddish? 88

Escape by three Scots, 120

Fruits of intermarriage, 23

Home for dinner, 68, 69
Hotel in Florida, 119
How can you tell the bride? 121
How do elephants make love in water? 123
How do you keep an elephant from charging? 124
How do you know when an elephant's in bed with you? 123
How many Blacks does it take? 128
How many JAPS does it take to screw in a light bulb? 128
How many Jewish mothers does it take? 128
How many Jews does it take to screw in a light bulb? 128
How many Marxists does it take? 128
How many Poles does it take to change a light bulb? 126
How many psychiatrists does it take? 128

If I sold shrouds, 99
Inheritance from the schnorrer, 107, 108

Janitor who married Bessie Cohen, 29
Jesus saves . . . , 113
Jew and the Nazi, 78
Jewish football yell, 113
Jewish logic, 17, 18
Jew on the Train, 138, 139

Lesson in arithmetic, 28
Life is like a glass of tea, 100
Lost key in Chelm, 72
Luncheon of Jewish ladies, 147

Matzos as literature, 77
Minding my own business, 74, 75
Mr. Cohen, I presume? 21, 22
My son, the President, 116

Index of Jokes

Name change for Mr. Katzman, 66, 67
Negro from Harvard, 54
New Catholic, 118
New joke at convention of comedians, 59
Next time I'll hold out for a mink coat, 129
No dancing allowed, 9

On not being born, 159
On the origin of Jewish noses, 116

Paradise and Hell, 130
Pleasure from my son, xii, xiii
Pope and the rabbi, 78, 79

Question of growing, 73
Question of relativity, xiv

Rabbi's advice, 99, 100
Rabbi's son and the shiksa, 21
Rabbi Who Ate Oysters, 143
Redneck in New York, 51, 52

Salmon and mayonnaise, 76
Shopping for brains, 126, 127
Sitting Shivah, 155, 156
Sometimes I think I'm my own worst enemy! 141

Tan in Miami, 57
Ten Commandments, 31
This is station KVY, Tel Aviv, 114
Threat by the schlimazel, 99
Trophy in the den, 55
Trotsky telegram, 39
Two bees, 8
Two Finns decide to go drinking, 157
Two Jews who see two schvartses, 157
Two ties, 75

Ugly thing, 55

What did Mr. Mink give Mrs. Mink for Christmas? 114
What did the elephant say? 124
What do you call a Jewish boy who can't stand the sight of blood? 115
What happened when Israel declared war on Egypt? 122

What happened when the Jewish woman took Thalidomide? 117
What has an IQ of 450? 126
What is harder than getting? 124
What is Polish matched luggage? 126
What is Red, Yellow, Orange, Green . . . ? 121
What is the smallest book? 122
What's the definition of a CPA? 115
What's the difference between a saloon and an Elephant fart? 123
What's the difference between Israelis and Italians? 122
What the elephant said to the naked man, 125
When Billy Graham sang . . . , 113
Who shot the five bullets that killed Mussolini? 122
Who's Pregnant at Jewish weddings? 140
Who wears a long, dirty white flowing robe? 121
Who won the Italian beauty contest? 122
Who won the Polish beauty contest? 126
Why are Jews optimists? 146
Why does the Pope have TGIF? 126
Why do Italians wear pointed shoes? 121
Why do Italian tanks? 122
Why don't Italians Kill Flies? 121
Why is the Polish suicide rate so low? 126
World's richest synagogue, 43, 44

Yankeleh's ploy, 45, 46
Yom Kippur, 66
You don't have to whisper, 102, 103
You're right! 6, 7

ABOUT THE AUTHOR

Arthur Asa Berger is a professor of Broadcast & Electronic Communication Arts at San Francisco State University, where he has taught since 1965. He is the author of numerous articles and books on media, popular culture, humor, and related concerns. Among his recent books are *An Anatomy of Humor*, *Blind Men and Elephants: Perspectives on Humor*, and *Cultural Criticism*. His book *Essentials of Mass Communication Theory* was awarded *Choice* magazine's Academic Book of the Year for 1996. He is Film and Television Review editor for *Society* magazine, a consulting editor of *Humor* magazine, and edits a series of book reprints, Classics in Communications, for Transaction Publishers. He has appeared on *The Today Show* and *20/20* and is frequently on radio and television in San Francisco. He is married, has two children, and lives in Mill Valley, California.